young, educated & BROKE

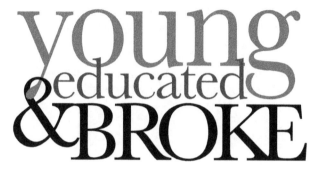

young educated &BROKE

An Introduction to America's New Poor

JAMIE BORROMEO

With Contributions from Eric A. Ochoa

NEW YORK

young, educated & BROKE
An Introduction to America's New Poor

Published in New York, New York, by Morgan James Publishing. Morgan James and The Entrepreneurial Publisher are trademarks of Morgan James, LLC.
www.MorganJamesPublishing.com

The Morgan James Speakers Group can bring authors to your live event. For more information or to book an event visit The Morgan James Speakers Group at www.TheMorganJamesSpeakersGroup.com.

ISBN 978-1-63047-089-0 paperback
ISBN 978-1-63047-090-6 eBook
ISBN 978-1-63047-091-3 hardcover
Library of Congress Control Number:
2014933827

A free eBook edition is available with the purchase of this print book.

CLEARLY PRINT YOUR NAME ABOVE IN UPPER CASE

Instructions to claim your free eBook edition:
1. Download the BitLit app for Android or iOS
2. Write your name in **UPPER CASE** on the line
3. Use the BitLit app to submit a photo
4. Download your eBook to any device

Cover Design by:
Rachel Lopez
www.r2cdesign.com

Interior Design by:
Bonnie Bushman
bonnie@caboodlegraphics.com

Photographs by:
Adam Von Mack Paris Photography
Alloria Winters Photography
Kevin Hofer San Francisco Photography

In an effort to support local communities, raise awareness and funds, Morgan James Publishing donates a percentage of all book sales for the life of each book to Habitat for Humanity Peninsula and Greater Williamsburg.

Get involved today, visit
www.MorganJamesBuilds.com

Habitat for Humanity
Peninsula and
Greater Williamsburg
Building Partner

This book is dedicated to all the Millennials
in America and around the globe.
I love my generation as much as I love this country.
To the Fire Goddess Pele: Thank you for igniting my heart.

A hui hou, mahalo nui loa.
(Until we meet again, thank you very much.)

Contents

Acknowledgments

When I embarked on this project, I didn't really know what I was asking for. It took a village to write this book, and I am so grateful to the many friends and family who created an environment for me to give birth to these ideas. I've shared such a big part of my heart with readers, and that is only because the following people shared their heart with me:

To all the Millennials who submitted testimonials, those who allowed me to publish your story and others who simply gave me insight into the lives of our generation: Thank you for clearing up the record for young people everywhere—for making the unseen, seen; for making the invisible, visible.

To my literary attorney, Denise Gibbon of Above the Dotted Line, whom I call my "Literary Angel": Thank you for your guidance without which this process would not have even been possible.

To the Morgan James publishing team: Thank you for this partnership and for giving me the opportunity to tell this story to the world.

To Stuart Grady, Joseph "Joe Grande" Lopez, Ann Darmola, Sonja Montgomery, Ed Nemetz, Daniel Roubian, Gloria Brosky, Susan Rasky, Sylvia Gex, Sonya Dukes, Michael Synn, Tam Nguyen, Rachel Rola, Raziel Arciega, Brian Tippens, Scott Vowels, Sonu Ratra, Gia Ly, Ken Duong, Bele Nguyen, Sally Starr, Charles Filius, the trio, Odette, Leila, and Elizabeth, to Humpy's Kona, James and Sandoz Maurer, Jason Leau, Tonic Heaukulani, Kolo Pa'akonia, Kapi'olani Mahoney, Colonel Dave Bateman, Dr. Cliff Kopp, Victoria Kalman, Mitch Tam, Rotary Club Kona Sunrise, Tracy Fosso from West Hawaii Today, The Wave 92FM, Habitat For Humanity West Hawaii, Diana Bertsch of World Championship Event IRONMAN, YogaBody Chino Hills, Adam Von Mack, my Washington D.C. network, the City of San Jose, the Vietnamese Chamber of Commerce, Congresswoman Judy Chu, Congressman Honda, the folks on the "Blue Carpet," to my editors at Split-Seed, and the GenerationDrive founding board members—thank you for your friendship, support and love.

Thank you to the GenerationDrive models: Ade Gibbs, Christina Booth, Marcus Allen Henderson, Molly Yee, Jessica Flores, and Shaelenn Hlinka. To Kevin Hofer Photography and his team of hair, makeup and wardrobe stylists; you've given a beautiful face to the Millennial generation.

To Sophia Khan, my sister, my confidant and my friend: I will always remember the generosity of you and your family. Thank you to your two very special brothers, Ali and Kareem, for making me your adopted sister. A big hug to Amir & Isma.

To my nieces Addison, Ziva, Brooklyn, and Dior and my nephews Branden, Tristan, Jayson, Logan, Jorden, Landen, Ayden, and Avery: I write every word of this book with you kids in mind. I wrote it so that the future is brighter, not only for this generation, but for yours. Tita Jamie loves you all so very much.

To my childhood best friends, Jennifer Stevenson, Stephanie Buenaventura, Nicole Aguila and Kristen Ludwick: I've watched some of you walk down the aisle, spent nights in delivery rooms with you and sat by you through life's greatest moments. Despite having to miss some of the milestones due to the nature of the traveling this book required of me, I appreciate you all for supporting me every step of the way.

To my sisters, Nicole Chang and Veronica Oliver: Thank you for sharing a childhood of the 80s with me that I can write in fondness of today. I love you both.

To my Mom and Dad whom I write so much about: You clearly have shaped much of who I am. Thank you for teaching me the gift of entrepreneurship. You were my true mentors, in both life and business. I am eternally grateful for both of you.

To Lolo and Lola: Thank you for giving me the spiritual tools necessary to navigate through this world. Thank you for epitomizing the love of God through your relationship with each other—it has provided a stable upbringing that I would be lost without.

To Eduardo and Holly: Thank you for your generosity, graciousness and support for Eric and me through the writing of this book. You have opened your hearts and your home to me in which I was able to spend many days on this manuscript. Eduardo, I thank you for your invaluable knowledge that you share in the interview contained in this book.

To my editor, my partner, and my best friend, Eric Ochoa: This book would not have been possible without your developmental editing, trips to the grocery store to buy me gelato on deadline, and your generous heart that allowed me the time and space to work on the manuscript. More importantly, your contributions and research on the rising income inequality in America and our shared desire to reverse the trend of poverty in our country gives voice to those who have none. For that and so much more, I love you.

Last but not least, to my dog, Bailey: Our 5K runs together, your incessant need for love and belly rubs, your eagerness to see me every time I come home brings me the comfort that only woman's best friend can bring.

Preface

Born to a prize-winning poet in New Zealand, world musical artist, Lorde, dominated the airwaves in the United States in the fall of 2013 with her chart-topping single "Royals." At the young age of 16, Lorde's lyrics were a reflection on her observations of the consumer culture that is promoted in some of the *Top 40* Billboard songs and hip-hop lyrics she grew up with. Lorde couldn't help but notice the disconnect between her life in Aukland as a normal teenager and the sentiments in hip-hop lyrics. In an interview, Lorde bluntly states, "When I wrote 'Royals,' I was listening to a lot of rap, but also a lot of Lana Del Rey, because she's obviously really hip-hop influenced, but all those references to expensive alcohol, beautiful clothes and beautiful cars—I was thinking, 'This is so opulent, but it's also bulls**t.'"

America's young people, known as Generation Y, or more popularly—Millennials—couldn't get enough of the teen sensation's message, which was made clear when Lorde won a Grammy for Song of the Year. The message was this: Our lives today look nothing like hip-hop videos. We'll never own the "*Cristal, Maybach, diamonds on your timepiece . . . Jet planes, islands, tigers on a gold leash . . . ,*" but, as the song continues, " *. . . We don't care. We aren't caught up in your love affair.*"

"It's a pointed rejection of the aspirations that have been foisted on the victims of capitalism," *Time* writer Douglas Walk says.

We are at a time where a sputtering U.S. economy and a slow recovery from the Great Recession have not allowed young people the ability to pursue the shared national ethos of prosperity and success with consistency. This was once known as the American Dream. Lorde's counter-culture song, which has achieved commercial success, means America's young people might be trying to tell the world something: We don't own anything. We have no jobs. We can't buy cars or houses, and we have a lot of student loan debt. We're educated. We're broke. And we have become America's new and invisible poor. Masked by the ability to, at the very least, live in Mom and Dad's basement and still eat from the refrigerators of extended families across America, we have food and shelter, but it isn't our own. We talk like educated people because we have a diploma, but that exceedingly expensive diploma has not translated into dollars in our bank accounts.

We were offered a version of the American Dream that we can't obtain. Post-recession, we've sought "life, liberty and the pursuit of happiness"—but in areas that have little to do with material objects. So, maybe it's time to redefine what that means since the essential tool in achieving the current version of the American Dream—money—is at a scarcity: unavailable in an anemic job market and a financial system at a halt. Maybe it's time to look at the reality of the consumer-driven world we have created—without the use of some pharmaceutical drug to numb us. However boring, painful, anxious, fearful or sad it makes us, many of us young people are ready for solutions and *real* change; not change vainly proposed to us through political campaigns, but change that gets us access and opportunity to live our version of the American

Dream. We can't get to the other side of this without looking at the cold, hard truth. We have to craft a different dialogue, one that is uniquely Millennial, which means it should be meaningful and innovative, educated and honest. And most importantly, we should use technology to start that dialogue.

That dialogue—for me at least—begins here . . .

Starting the
Real Conversation

*"Every worthwhile accomplishment, big or little, has its stages of
drudgery and triumph: a beginning, a struggle, and a victory."*
—Mahatma Gandhi

The definition of the Millennial Generation: Generation Y. Close to
a third of all Americans. Seventy-eight million strong. Born between
1980–2000. Millennials are known by some as "the lost generation."
Referred to as spoiled, lazy, entitled, and "special little snowflakes."
Millennials are often stereotyped as narcissists who are over-praised and
coddled; given trophies and gold stars for practically every achievement
since birth.

However true you believe these stereotypes to be, there is no denying
this fact: Millennials are the future. Millennials are the next generation
of business leaders, career professionals, and consumers. You are either

hiring a Millennial or selling to a Millennial. Equally important, in the next few decades, Millennials are the future caregivers of the largest generation to retire in history—the Baby Boomers—who are those born between 1946 and 1964.

I am a Millennial who graduated from college during what Harvard University's Lawrence F. Katz calls, in more technical terms, "The most severe . . . labor market downturn since the Great Depression in the 1930s."

According to a testimonial provided by Mr. Katz to the Joint Economic Committee in Congress on April 29, 2010, the Great Recession's long-term unemployment consequences disproportionately affected young workers.

The plethora of Baby Boomers I've spoken to address youth unemployment in passing or dismissively, when I believe this issue should matter to all Americans.

Why?

Well, I believe long-term unemployment and underemployment of young workers will have dire effects on the future of our economy and the retirement of our parents. It is happening during a time where the largest generation to retire in the history of our country will be cared for—primarily by the Millennials—the largest generation to ever go through an economic collapse of this magnitude.

Here is the downside for those looking into retirement: Since January 1, 2011, every day more than 10,000 Baby Boomers will reach the age of 65. For the next 19 years, this trend will continue on a daily basis. This means we need to produce capable American leaders to fill the positions of power our parents and grandparents will soon be vacating.

Key words: *Capable American Leaders.*

With declining educational attainment and skyrocketing student loan debt, how do we become capable? With jobs going overseas, how do we keep leadership American? And without careers, how do young people gain the experience, the network, or the resources to become the leaders necessary to occupy all these positions that will become vacant in the years to come?

More bad news: No capable American leaders mean there will be no Social Security for Boomers.

35% of Americans already above the age of 65 rely almost solely on Social Security payments for income. According to a report by the Bureau of Labor & Statistics in August 2012, unemployment remained at 22.8% for 18 and 19 year olds, 12.4% for 20 to 24 year olds, and 8.1% for 25 to 34 year olds. And, depending on which polling firm you got statistics from, young people hover between 15–20% unemployment rates when accounting for those going to school.

All in all, this could mean that America will continue to empty the Social Security piggy bank while fewer citizens are paying into the system, which could leave our middle-class retiring parents in dire straits.

The downside that our generation has to look forward to, historically, is that long-term unemployment has led to large declines in average earnings, severe health problems, and mortality increases from extended unemployment. This glaring reality cannot be good news for the young people going through it—or the generation retiring—since parents, grandparents, and great grandparents would like a cushy (or at least poverty-free) retirement, and their kids off their couch.

Full House, once a favorite show of children in the 90's, has taken on a whole new meaning in the 21st century. Twenty-two million young people are still living with their parents. Young people can't afford homes, can't find jobs, and at this rate, the vast majority frankly feel like they have no clue what is happening.

According to *Forbes Magazine*, which published an article in October 2012 on this topic, "Adult children are taking a toll on their boomer parents. Nearly 50% of parents with children between ages 18 to 39 are supporting them financially in various ways including living expenses, transportation costs, spending money, medical bills and help with paying loans like student loan debt."

What's more, according to one recent survey, 36% of Americans say that they don't contribute anything at all to retirement savings. So while the Baby Boomers are still taking care of their adult children into their retirement, they will have to figure out how to save more to take care of both generations.

So, how do we get parents to stop paying for their adult children if their adult children can't find jobs or full-time work?

The statistical reality of this phenomenon does not tell the whole story. The numbers do not account for people like me, who are not financially supported by their parents. Some of us were considered underemployed, and others were employed at the time of the recession, but barely making it. Because I was working, I could not be included in the unemployment or underemployment figures. Even though I worked hard to obtain my Bachelor of Arts degree from a respected university, I had credit card bills that were sky high, rent that consumed more than half of my paycheck, and food costs that went up roughly 4% annually. I was paying for all of these expenses and more on a ten dollar an hour salary working front desk jobs at high-end hotels or working a hostess position at a restaurant. Multiply my situation by millions of Millennials, and you have an entire generation that is burning to see this economic recovery through. We were, and still are, an educated, talented and depressed collective—wondering when we can finally leave Mom and Dad's house to start our adult lives.

My Millennial Story

I was, at one time, in a position where I had to work three different jobs to ensure I could pay rent. Mounting problems from the economic collapse put such a strain on my parents' relationship that they split up in 2008. That year, our family small business went belly-up in the recession. Due to skyrocketing healthcare costs, we couldn't cover my mother's medical expenses after her health insurance was denied for "pre-existing conditions" from the lupus she was diagnosed with nearly a decade before. Due to these expensive healthcare costs, and the toll it took on our personal lives from our hurting business, we were part of the first wave of foreclosures before the peak of the economic crisis. At that point, there were no government regulations that encouraged banks to negotiate with Main Street Americans like my family. I lost my home a few months after graduating from college. My condo was auctioned on the Santa Cruz courthouse steps. Only those who have had to endure this will understand the kind of heartbreak and insecurity that comes from losing your home in such a traumatic way.

During the same period of 2007, I was offered the opportunity to be a special student speaker at my graduation while, ironically, my last quarter's tuition was in collections. I didn't know if tuition would be paid at the time because of the financial burden my parents were going through. The successive foreclosures of all their properties had them too preoccupied to call the registrar back, given the simultaneous nature of our financial burdens. Two days before graduation, I was hospitalized from a nervous breakdown. However, I did manage to make it to graduation and deliver a speech on this exact topic, and years later, that speech I delivered on graduation day has served as a source of inspiration for writing this book.

I can't tell you how many nervous breakdowns I had that year. Or how many times I couldn't have cared less if I drove off a cliff on Highway 17 in Santa Cruz, California. That economic crisis was my rock bottom, and my life since then has been me climbing up.

The economic recovery took so long that my peers and I were no longer in the 18–24 age demographic. We had transitioned to the 25–30 age demographic while still within the same recession—never having achieved more than an unpaid internship.

Keeping that in mind, it's clear that dividing these two age groups does a huge disservice to finding solutions for alleviating young Americans' high unemployment and underemployment rates at this time. Putting us in an older age group masks the reality of the job crisis the "young, entitled" Millennials have endured the past several years, and it makes things look like they are getting better when really, we've just re-arranged the furniture on the Titanic.

Hiding out in the university system has become the new safe haven for twenty-somethings—a hideout that has contributed to Millennials' staggering student loan debt. In the U.S., a total of one trillion dollars and an average of $45,000 of total debt per capita are being carried on the backs of young people. Some of the only impressive numbers from Millennials you'll see in this anemic economy are the astounding student loan debt and the endless number of unpaid internships—which Millennials feel privileged to have. Steven Hill, author of *10 Steps to Repair American Democracy*, writes, "Young people are using higher education to escape a rocky job market." He says unemployment statistics "fail to account for the millions of young people either attending university or in vocational training programs" and "undermines the unemployment rate's credibility." This means, not only are unemployment numbers still high for Millennials, but analysts are not even getting the whole picture from the Bureau of Labor and Statistics, since the student population is not accounted for in the methodology of unemployment rates.

Dr. Meg Jay wrote *The Defining Decade*, and she says, "80 percent of life's most significant events take place by age 35," with the most definitive years in our 20s.

The scary truth is that I actually believe she is right. If her hypothesis is that the twenty-something years are the most definitive in a person's life, then my graduating class is on year nine of that decade. I believe my generation attempted to address the myriad of issues I discuss in this book through the Occupy Wall Street movement, but the momentum fizzled within the first year.

The biggest criticism of the Occupy Wall Street movement was that it didn't have a solid agenda. Critics said, "That's so Millennial. Freethinkers. Giving people room to share their ideas. A collective movement without strategic objectives. Just a bunch of kids with tents outside of Wall Street with no tangible asks for the people who have the power to make decisions." It looked like an inability to draft a plan of action that properly asked for deliverables was allowing the fat cats on Wall Street and the leaders in Washington to silence us. But I believe Occupy Wall Street was a smashing success for this reason: Most Americans now know about widening income inequality. Most Americans now know there is a top one percent and that they aren't in it. Occupy Wall Street gave people like me a platform to get deeper into conversations that affect middle class Americans. In the case of this analysis, Occupy Wall Street gave me the opportunity to create awareness around what I call "America's New Poor."

Who This Book Is For

I could describe all the problems I encountered during that economic catastrophe, but that would be as futile as counting all the stars in the sky. I have no intention of making this a sob story of a Millennial, nor a cry for help for someone to rescue my generation out of the depths of our despair. There is a certain kind of wake-up call that grief brings to you, which I believe expedites the learning process. I believe grief was my teacher. My lessons were learned immediately upon receiving the course material, and like a good student, I mastered many things that year that allow me to tell you the story with such a different energy: one of hope, one of perseverance, one of unshakable faith that Americans have what it takes to continue on the long road of greatness ahead of us. But none of that would have been possible if I did not receive mentoring and sound advice from generations that came before me. In learning their different insights, I was able to find the complimentary angles between their perspectives and the Millennial perspective in problem solving. I found my beacons of hope in mentors—members of older generations that had leadership positions. They voluntarily came down from their ivory tower, and at certain points felt a patriotic duty to ensure the next generation had the survival skills for this financial Armageddon the youth were thrust into.

If I never encountered diverse opinions of how to see my way out of the darkness in my personal life, I would have never become a successful entrepreneur. The innovative solutions I found in my career and personal life through an intergenerational problem-solving approach helped me to understand the problems, and more importantly, the solutions, much better than I could have if I only sought counsel from those my own age. Learning from the wisdom passed on from my mentors, I found the necessary perspective on how resilient the American people really are.

Although my life on the exterior looked like it was falling apart, I was coming together in my mind and my heart. I had people all around me that gave me hope and inspiration even through my darkest hours. It gave me faith that the lessons I learned were beyond the experience. I believe you cannot find a solution if you do not understand the problem. There is no better teacher than pain, and I have transformed that pain into passion. And my passion is to help be a part of the solution and fix things in cooperation with those who suffered in some way during the Great Recession.

Millennials as New Members of America's Poor

What these challenging experiences did was give young Americans a glimpse at what life is like for the entrenched poor. Poverty, underserved communities, and a lack of resources have plagued other groups of people throughout our country's history. As America's New Poor, we have one advantage that many members of the entrenched poor do not: We have a high rate of college graduates. Because of this luxury, I believe it is the social obligation of Millennials to use our knowledge to advocate for Americans that lack significant access to economic opportunities.

Millennials were dubbed "The Trophy Kids" by talking heads because we were raised to be a self-confident, heavily praised group. But the problem is not that we were heavily praised, the problem is the unproductive and misinformed stereotypes offered for us. All those labels do is prohibit us from shining. Instead of criticizing us, I believe a more productive solution is to understand our unique talents. This is a plea to put our talents to work by providing a pipeline on our quest for what—to many—is a forgotten American Dream. Beyond acknowledging that we too would like a seat at the table to solve some of our generation's most pressing challenges; we actually want decision-makers to *put us to work* in a way where we can be a part of our country's solution.

Yes, the mainstream conversation has talked about Millennials, but I don't believe it's been a two-sided conversation, and therefore it's not a *real* conversation. There have been generalizations made about a group of people that totals 70-plus million in population. I don't believe that the media has covered this generation in such a positive light. This isn't about pouring pink paint over the conversation about us either—but if we do not have a different dialogue to balance the mainstream discussion, then we will continue to be sorely misunderstood. What you choose to label something is important in defining the problem and finding a solution; clearing up the record for Millennials is absolutely essential if we are to move forward as a nation.

To be clear this book does not focus just on Millennials—it is about offering insights to anyone from any generation who is interested in becoming a part of the recovery movement. I know our generation can be useful in helping other generations out of their misery and sorrow. Every generation suffered through this recession—so this is not about focusing solely on Millennials because we were not the only ones affected. More so, there is so much ground to cover in addressing our issues, that I had to limit the discussion to what I believe would be most productive to a solutions-based conversation. For the first time in the history of our country, we have four generations in the workforce. In a crowded job market, Millennials are inherently going to occupy leadership positions when more Baby Boomers retire, so, in the interest of having a conversation about the future of America, an examination of Millennials can help other generations prepare for what's ahead. I include a myriad of issues—from the political climate in Washington to lack of education reforms in the U.S.—that have contributed to a generation that is getting a late start on fundamental skills that will prepare us for a new frontier in the global economy. These problems require all hands on deck and an expedited discussion so we can move forward in action.

Whether a member of the Silent Generation (1925–1942), the Baby Boomers (1946–1964), Generation X (1965–1980), or if you are a Millennial, this book is for you. This is meant to be an intergenerational discussion. I will give tangible evidence and statistics to highlight the useful nature of Millennials in all areas of life, ranging anywhere from discussion on the innovative industries that can give rise to a whole new crop of entrepreneurs and business leaders to personal development and the health of our bodies. I believe we can utilize my peer group, alongside other generations, to restore America back to its greatness in numerous parts of society. I feel the passion and faith of U.S. citizens are the strongest weapons in their arsenal to attack the status quo at this juncture in American history.

Speeding Up the Recovery

I was fed up with the job market, so once I turned 25, I started my first company to take control of my own financial destiny. I was self-taught and had very little professional training. I consider myself somewhat successful, however, no one should have to work *that* hard or have to experience the learning curve so fast just to pay the bills. Any starving artist knows it takes a toll on your health, your sanity, and overall well-being.

The great part about it was, despite all the bleak numbers being reported, I was still able to provide a job for myself. I was contributing to the economy through innovation and motivating myself to go beyond the statistics to create the financial freedom I desired. If I was given more support, a road map, or even an investor that was willing to extend a hand, I don't believe all the emotional and mental baggage would have had to come with it.

Even with flaws in their analysis, statistical data reports 5.5 million young people are unemployed, and, unfortunately, many of them will not have the same opportunity I did to open a business, because they lack the fundamental skills necessary to run their own company.

I want to change that for my generation, especially since in Mr. Katz' testimonial, he said we would need to create 14.9 million new jobs by January 2014 to make up for the current job losses and absorb the 0.8 percent per year average labor force growth projected by the Department of Labor. January 2014 came and went, and we certainly did not see 14.9 million jobs created.

So what is the best way to create jobs?

Teach people how to create their *own* jobs.

I write this book in the hope that it might spur some discussion between the current leadership and Millennials all over the world to become part of an entrepreneurial and workforce development movement. I truly believe that the best way to create jobs is to teach people how to create their own, and to train a new workforce to provide services in emerging industries. I write in hopes that one day, when I do have children, they won't ever have to feel the kind of despair I did at 21 years old. It was a wonderful time of lessons, but the level of pain and duration of pain my generation and I had is certainly unnecessary. This economic crisis was due in part to man-made problems that could have had man-made solutions, if only our public policy makers and leaders would have looked ahead far enough to see it coming. Also, they could have focused on solutions like entrepreneurship and the intergenerational involvement of established professionals systematically mentoring their younger counterparts to solve the challenges that were ahead.

I am a fan of the concept of a collective consciousness. I believe that, imbedded in the hearts and minds of Millennials, not just in America—but globally—there is an invisible thread that ties our shared experiences together to weave the perfect solutions. In raising awareness around the aforementioned problems that I believe have been put on the back-burner for far too long, a discussion that the collective can sink their teeth into is what our generation craves. This is why I have included testimonials from Millennials who have a diverse set of experiences shedding light on solutions. I hope this book can be a voice that adds depth to the understanding and experience of the reader, and offers a glimpse of living testaments of hope through the lives of other young people. If we give young, displaced workers opportunities to transition to new jobs, teach new workforce development skills, offer entrepreneurship training in numbers, and teach financial literacy to the next generation, we can recover by combining forces with the current leadership to provide intergenerational cooperation and solutions. Because we will have to pay off the debt of the generations before us, and address the bad policy decisions made on our behalf, I do believe there is no better time than now to get started.

A Word on the Purpose and Structure of This Book

I write this book to break the relative silence from our generation on these subjects. I am a singular voice in a sea of young people proposing a draft of ideas—a blueprint, if you will—for Millennials. It is written simply as a series of reflections on certain topics, which occurred in different locations around the world that I visited through seven years of my personal, financial, spiritual, and emotional recovery. While much of my book contains observations on the young people of my generation, the journey I describe is deeply personal and is focused mostly on my self-exploration. My American Dream has become a dream for the world to discover themselves and to discover their fundamental connection with each other, hopefully revealing a desire to assist those without material advantages.

The structure of this book is written as part memoir, part social commentary. I kept the format of these musings as close to stream of consciousness as possible, in order to portray accurately the thought process of Millennials. It's honest, and sometimes, I use profanity. It is in no way meant to offend or be crass; it is a counterweight to the lies we've been told through mass marketing, over-commercialization, and a generational obsession with consumerism. In keeping with the authenticity of my message of truth, I am as honest in my writing as possible. Topics might also make older generations, let's say a little dizzy. In a culture that encouraged multi-tasking and a fast-pace in the way we talk and walk, writing is no different. As a form of communication, I communicate as authentically Millennial as I can. The subjects included are covered in this text in bite-sized chunks of information because this is the way information is encouraged to be digested and expressed by Millennials. This phenomenon is most clearly demonstrated through social media sites like Twitter that don't allow you to tweet more than 160 characters at a time. This communication style can also be seen in text messages, Facebook, iChat, and other text communication. The subject matter changes frequently from paragraph to paragraph in the same way that a Millennial's mind must transition among a myriad of concerns. Any shift in tenses is intentional and has a purpose. Any interviews conducted, e-mails, or conversations from Millennials or those who provided testimonial are strictly anonymous and are not necessarily my views, however, I did find it relevant to include these voices to show the diversity in opinion of how we should go about finding solutions for America.

With that said, it is time for young people to energize our country and stand alongside the generations that came before us, but with a sense of our own unique purpose. There is no better time to start this personal journey than now.

CHAPTER 1

Silicon Valley, 2007:
We are the 99%

"A pessimist sees the difficulty in every opportunity; an optimist sees the opportunity in every difficulty."

—Winston Churchill

My palms were sweaty.

I was rehearsing my lines in my head as the dean of the college was speaking to our graduating class. I was a college senior from the University of California, Santa Cruz. I found myself chosen as the student speaker for the graduation ceremony, and for the first time in my life, I was nervous to speak at the podium.

At a young age, I was groomed to speak publicly. My mom and dad hosted corporate events and political fundraisers around the country regularly, so they had no problem handing me the microphone when

I was twelve years old. The podium was like an old friend. I could do everything from telling audience members who were corporate CEOs and high-profile community leaders to "please enjoy the dessert" to telling jokes while the audio/visual teams fixed technical difficulties.

An unlikely candidate in the past to speak on behalf of such a liberal, hippie college, I was both thrilled and anxious to represent the Class of 2007. I had grown up a conservative Catholic, but after attending UC Santa Cruz, I had opened my mind to a different way of looking at the world. After four years of exposure to the principles of the university, I embodied what UC Santa Cruz had taught me: to embrace the environment, appreciate diversity, and to have an open, free exchange of ideas within my community and to be of service to society.

I honestly wouldn't have even applied among hundreds of candidates for student speaker at the commencement ceremony if it weren't for one of my former journalism professors. A year before graduation, I had participated in the University of California DC (District of Columbia) program and took a journalism class. My professor was Dr. Susan Rasky, who was nothing short of an inspiration. After taking her class, she wanted me to apply for the journalism program at University of California, Berkeley, where she taught. She said, "You are one of the best writers I've ever had." I was so honored to get such kudos from a seasoned journalist. After kindly rejecting the notion that I could one day be a professional writer, I at least took her up on the idea that I could speak on behalf of my graduating class.

So, back on stage for the graduation speech, it was quite shocking that I was the least bit nervous. There were about a thousand people looking out at me, so surely this was my biggest audience yet. But I don't think it was the amount of people that frightened me; it was the content of my speech, which felt like a prophetic revelation, which scared me.

In preparation for the speech, the graduation committee had asked me to add a more hopeful tone to it so I could energize and inspire the crowd. My speech was energizing and inspiring—but I also wanted it to be honest. I could not speak of hope without highlighting the candid troubles of my generation—troubles that had yet to materialize when I spoke the words.

The majority of my peers were still unaware that, in a few months, the whole U.S. economy would be brought to its knees, crushing the spirits and economic opportunities of my graduating class. But I knew better. I read too many articles, watched the news too much, and interacted far too often with corporate and government leaders to think anything else. We were the first class to graduate into what was to become the Great Recession, and my speech was an omen of the events that were soon to come.

I don't blame my generation for not knowing. I think the only reason I was aware was because I started to notice a funny thing that happened during my last year of college. Every time I turned on the news, I would see connections between the state of the country and my personal experiences (and they were not positive). A report on mounting national debt would be on the local news station. Then, minutes later, a debt collector would call me about a late credit card payment. I'd turn on the TV the next day and listen to the news on the war in Iraq, and that same day when the mail carrier would drop off my mail, I would read a letter from an old high school friend who wrote pages and pages from the desert, talking about how much he missed the simple comforts of home—like sleeping in a bed. Politicians on Capitol Hill would argue about a proposal in Congress to keep Americans on health plans despite pre-existing conditions, while my mother would call frantically that same day to tell me she was denied by health insurance companies for her own pre-existing conditions. I would hear a news network feature a panel of experts regarding this new phenomenon of staggering student loan debt, while simultaneously, I was scared I wouldn't graduate because I couldn't pay my college tuition.

Were my experiences a mirror of the larger issues we were facing as a nation? Was my experience a microcosm of the societal issues that were plaguing the country? From that moment on, I realized I might have become a poster-child for challenging topics discussed in the national discourse.

The Land of Technology: Silicon Valley

Weeks after the crowds cleared the bleachers and the stage was empty, I went on as an official graduate and moved to Silicon Valley. I liked Silicon Valley for two very distinct reasons. One, Silicon Valley liked young people. It appreciated the knowledge we had to offer, and everything in its culture embraced younger generations. Two, I liked that innovation was the name of the game in town. To innovate, to use technology, and to promote entrepreneurship were key characteristics of the culture that made me a proud resident of the area.

I worked for the City of San Jose, known as the "Capital of Silicon Valley" for a time, then I interned for a Congressional member who represented Silicon Valley, and shortly thereafter I ran a national non-profit headquartered in Mountain View—home to many technology companies like Google, Mozilla, Symantec and Intuit. In only two years, I had produced a half-million dollar budget for the organization and was working with corporations like Apple, Lockheed Martin Space Systems, and other respected *Fortune 500* companies. This platform allowed me to work closely with community organizers, corporations, and political campaigns.

What I noticed the most about Silicon Valley was the obvious love for technology. And young people were leading the charge with it.

As a generation for whom iPads, Smartphones and computers had become everyday household items, our techno-literacy awed the older generations. The ability for online messages to spread like wildfire gave rise to a new crop of celebrities, personalities, talking heads, and experts. A good example of how this technological shift altered our culture is pop-sensation Justin Bieber, and his rise to fame, which came from the millions of hits he received on his YouTube channel and videos.

From the passionate community organizer to the candidate for public office, messages, speeches and virtual meet-ups could now be formed through Facebook—the world's most popular social media site, invented by Millennial Mark Zuckerberg. The ability to send a Tweet or photo using Instagram, SnapChat, or other social media sites to other countries around the world makes the Millennial Generation the first truly global generation in history. You can instant message your friends, fellow community organizers, or send out information to the whole world with the click of a mouse.

This was also the era that led to the rise of President Obama. Barack Obama's seat in the oval office was historic for more reasons than one. He was not only the first Black president our country elected into office—he was also the first presidential candidate to utilize a sophisticated social media strategy in a political campaign, which he did in 2008. Many experts believe this approach and execution was the key to his victory. In an article titled, "iPresident: How Social Media Shaped the Narrative of Barack Obama," the author says, "Obama's embrace of social media—utilizing social networks as a means of encouraging civic engagement—has allowed him to create a conversation, and often an open dialogue, with the public. He has created an environment of transparency never before experienced in American politics, a sort of new political ecology for the digital age."

Beyond grassroots organizing, relationships have been formed through social media in a way they previously had not been. One of my girlfriends met her husband on e-Harmony, a dating website. Old friends have reconnected, and loved ones are updated on the happenings of each other's lives through status updates on Facebook.

Commerce and international trade have dramatically improved as well. The World Wide Web connects countries and citizens byte by byte. If you have a product or service that has to be sent overseas, the exchange and transaction is much easier. Banking has become more efficient. ATM machines and electronic transfers take anywhere from a few seconds to a few days. Filing data, record keeping, research and information gathering have all improved because of technology.

Efficiencies have been created in academia that earlier generations could not have dreamed of. When I was invited to return to my old elementary school by my 6th grade teacher, Mrs. Brosky, to do a presentation to teach students the importance of writing, I was in awe of the technology that these young people had access to. Notebooks are now replaced with iPads. Old projectors are now replaced by high-tech MacBooks. Chalkboards are now replaced with LCD screens. The education environment is more interactive with the use of multimedia and electronic games, and teachers can now engage students with technology that makes learning fun.

As a generation that has had access to computer technology since birth, Millennials have grown up with a powerful technical resource available in a way that no previous generation has had. Global conversations, an exchange of information, and a new virtual ecology has created a new world for Millennials.

The Great Recession
But, with every great creation, comes a downside. The financial sector used technology to squeeze more and more money out of the economy until, what we now know as The Great Recession hit. Technology, like the Internet, computers, and bank transfers collectively gave way to Wall Street creating complicated financial instruments that turned simple things like mortgages into sophisticated investments to be speculated on. The banking industry structured each of these

mortgages into complex financial products like crafty engineers. Spiffy names like Structured Investment Vehicles (SIVs), Collateralized Debt Obligations (CDOs), Credit Default Swaps, Asset Backed Securities and Collateralized Mortgage Obligations (CMOs) created an alphabet soup that average Americans couldn't even take a sip of. The fact that it was so complicated contributed to people making such bad decisions on these investments. On top of that, let's not forget how globalization assisted in these efforts. Your mortgage was now a product that could be sold by financial institutions as an investment to virtually anyone in the world. They turned it into a security—something that can be bought like a Treasury Bill or Certificate of Deposit (CD).

As Wall Street categorized mortgages into "risk profiles" and "tranches," and gambled which American home would give the best bang for the buck (or what investors like to call "return on investment") the loans that everyday Americans used to purchase their house had now become just another item to play Russian Roulette with on Wall Street.

Let me explain in layman's terms what was happening with mortgages for the uninitiated. People qualified for different interest rates on their mortgages. There were people that qualify at levels from prime (market rate) down to subprime (worse than market rate). Wall Street turned these mortgages into something you could invest in, based on the grade of the mortgages. The riskier ones, which are subprime, gave the investor much bigger returns, and because speculative financial institutions love big returns, they were often willing to take the increased risks.

Then, they essentially sold shares of the security—which was composed of thousands of mortgages—as if it was shares of a stock, like it was a business. They ended up putting huge amounts of money into subprime mortgages, due to the comparatively higher return you could make on subprime mortgage-backed securities. So much so, that the banks had to get more Americans to take out mortgages so they could keep making money. The problem with that is not everyone made enough money to cover his or her mortgage payments. There's a reason they got *subprime* mortgages in the first place, after all. Many of these people started to default on their loans and began a chain reaction that eventually cascaded into the toppling of the U.S. economy.

A perfect storm of obsession with short-term profits by the financial industry and the cultural obsession of consumers wanting to own a home, a car, gadgets and technology made the economy collapse like a house of cards. I, myself, was certainly not immune to the dealings on Wall Street. Within six months of receiving my diploma, the Great Recession hit. My family had lost our wealth during the financial crisis, and my mom was diagnosed with lupus, which made it hard for her to work through all the turmoil.

My condo on River Street, in Santa Cruz, that my mother intended to be an investment property for me upon graduation, was auctioned on the courthouse steps after defaulting. I cried for a few days, then immediately had to find a place to stay. In the interim, I stayed with a friend and his family in Santa Clara, California.

The owner of the home was my friend's father, Ed. He was a Baby Boomer, a jolly man at over 300 pounds. Divorced with two adult children, he lived between his retreat home in the mountains and the house he commuted to in Silicon Valley to visit his sons. His diverse experiences made him an interesting man. He was sarcastic, witty, and funny as hell. I'd jokingly tell him that if he grew his beard any longer he'd start to look like Santa Claus. He was a small business owner who lived out what his generation knew as the American Dream. His mother and father emigrated from Croatia to provide a better life for Ed and his younger sister. They did, indeed, achieve that. The home where they lived, in which I was renting a room at the time, felt like a perfect 1960's home. It felt like your typical white-picket fence house with a perfectly manicured yard. As a small business owner, Ed's company provided car salespeople with customer satisfaction consulting. Uncle Ed would use behavioral sciences to analyze data on customer service. He had his own high-tech version of a call center based right out of his living room. He was a typical Silicon Valley entrepreneur—a man who created and innovated right out of his home and was able to retire with his financial needs met for his later years.

Ed had the uncanny ability to walk the line between interacting with the everyday Joe, which was his blue-collar client base and then, in his personal life, flip the script and analyze the world around him like an academic, providing sound esoteric musings like someone from a religious order while encouraging the "you-can-do-it spirit" like a basketball coach. All through my post-college blues, as I picked up the pieces of my life during the recession, Uncle Ed's dynamic spirit provided a bright light in my life.

On one not-so-special evening, we sat on the porch while he smoked a cigarette. His husky stature would make the bench creak multiple times. The rhythm between his puffs of smoke, creaking bench, and crickets outside brought a harmonious experience I craved at such an unsteady time in my life. In an unexpected moment amidst the everyday mundane, he said, "I should really quit this shit," as he'd put out his smoke. Then, I'd hear some prophetic words emerge from such a simple man. After moments of basking in the stillness and sounds of nature, amidst all this economic turmoil that America was going through, I couldn't help but ask him, "Ed, what do you think will happen to my generation? What is the fate of the next generation of professionals?"

I remember his words vividly.

Jamie, I am not sure my thinking regarding the next generation of professionals is relevant. What might be more important is how they see themselves in a society whereby market forces driven by corporate greed dominate public policy, and what do they intend to do about it? Will the can of economic reckoning be kicked down the road? Will young professionals accept the demand that they do more work and settle for less reward? The private sector of profit and greed will drain young professionals so that at the end of the workday they will collapse—exhausted—into their little residential side-by-side cubicles trying to catch their breath. Can they overcome the apathy of a comfortable couch coupled with a refrigerator of food like substances; an internet entertainment culture supplemented by mind numbing effects of alcohol or drugs? Will they organize to meet the future challenges of the environment, the economy, the nature of weapons of war, as the earth's dwindling supply of oil, gas and water increasingly become the subject of global conflict?

These sorts of concerns will determine the near future. I suspect most young professionals will shirk these cerebral headaches for a more practical survivor's mentality of just finding meaningful work, and be satisfied that they can manage to do that. They will probably try to fit economic strata much lower than was the case in the past. Given there is no basis for comparison, they will consider that level to be normal and acceptable. They will leave the big picture solutions to a select group of corporate and government elites to solve. The result will be changes that benefit the elite few who are driving the train, and everyone else will compete for the economic crumbs. Gated communities for personal security and the availability of bottled water due to contaminated aquifers will be the essence of what is left of the American Dream.

Government's role as purveyor of fair and balanced economic opportunity has been co-opted and rendered ineffective by monied corporate, banking, and military industrial interests and lobbyists. The tail is wagging the dog rather than the other way around. The White House is unable to move this private sector dragon, and any attempt at seeking relief there is naive with Obama, or any other elected President. Congress does not want to tame the private sector dragon because the body is designed to be obstructive, and there is a substantial lobbying effort to do nothing. The null option, or do-nothing approach, by design has significant outcomes that adversely affect young professionals. Local government is broke and is only trying to survive bankruptcy by scaling down basic services. If young professionals don't recognize this reality; then it is only because they lack the comparative viewpoint that experience and historical perspective provides. The quote from Hubert Humphrey resonates in my head, it goes something like: "You can judge a society by how it helps the young, cares for the old, and assists the disabled." You can see that our government takes care of oil and gas with subsidies, pharmaceuticals by not regulating, healthcare and insurance by not eliminating their scam, and the military-industrial complex to keep international trade corridors flowing. The educational system, subsidies for the poor, and Social Security we are told need to be cut back due to a lack of funding. Even a modest effort at healthcare reform has been stymied by corporate interests to keep their profits flowing.

Public policy is no longer made for the public good or benefit in most cases, or at least the ones that matter. For example, environment, tax laws, housing costs, healthcare, immigration, etcetera. We now get public policy that is most profitable with corporations competing with government at all levels for a dwindling supply of tax revenue. The American Dream of my generation is gone, and the shrinking size of the middle class is only a small by-product of an economy and culture based upon unregulated greed. I will spare you all the examples to support this premise, but just take a look at all the regulations placed on Wall Street to prevent another economic meltdown. The answer is zero!

We are now a nation built on debt and a corporate culture that will force young professionals to work harder for less in a market that has dwindling jobs, making it lucky for those that actually have them. Our greatest import will be the projection of our military around the world through our 300 bases laid out globally. I do not see the fundamental changes that need to happen occurring in our country. On the contrary, I see a situation that continues to deteriorate and erode the earning potential of young professionals. When I graduated with a Master's degree, there was no debt incurred, as the government subsidized the cost. This was considered normal. The first great debt of my generation was buying a house, and then beginning a family. Now young professionals graduate with soaring educational debt in a job market unable to accommodate them, and as a result approximately 40% must live with their parents while others work at Starbucks with their advanced degrees. This is an inhospitable economic climate for those whose families are unable to provide some postgraduate financial assistance. The very existence of this economic condition is proof that the standard financial starting point for the American Dream has been fundamentally denigrated to such a level that it is now a verbal cliché relegated in reality to a historical dustbin.

I would find myself reflecting for quite a few days about his rather lengthy monologue. I felt my generation at a crossroads. What created this? How did we allow it to get this bad? When did America fall asleep to the things that mattered, and how did we inherit this mess? I began to research the history of the Millennial.

Reaganomics

The decade I was born, the 1980s, marked the period of Reaganomics—the idea of trickle down-economics, embracing free-market principles and deregulation of private enterprise. The television became the new religion of young people throughout America. It was our babysitter, our entertainment, and our friend. Parents and critics started to resent the technology, as they felt they could control neither their kids' obsession with Saturday morning cartoons, nor the content that we Millennials were exposed to.

Frankly, parents did have a reason to be scared. Government was no longer "protecting small children from the barrage of commercialized programming brought about by broadcasting deregulation," as one children's rights group put it.

According to Britannica Encyclopedia, "The years of the administration of President Ronald Reagan were a time of intense deregulation of the broadcast industry. Mark Fowler and Dennis Patrick, both Federal Communications Commission (FCC) chairmen appointed by Reagan, advocated free-market philosophies in the television industry. Fowler frankly described modern television as a business rather than a service. In 1981, he stated 'television is just another appliance. It's a toaster with pictures.'" The fact that the people responsible for regulating television looked at it as no more significant or socially powerful than a toaster gives you a little idea as to how TV has had some negative impact. Without looking at any research or doing any studies, it is apparent that TV has had a massive impact on the worldview and cultural norms of the Millennial Generation. Should such a powerful tool of corporate America really be as deregulated as a toaster? Whether we agree with it or not, that is certainly what happened.

Mr. Fowler accelerated this deregulation from 1981–1987. The number of commissioners was reduced from five down to seven in those years. Media monopoly laws allowed for "single corporate owners, once limited to owning seven stations nationally to . . . [now own up to] 12 stations." TV stations extended their license periods from three years to five years, and "the 1949 Fairness Doctrine, which charged stations with scheduling time for opposing views on important controversial issues, was eliminated."

In an article further exploring this media monopoly, titled, "Babes in the Marketplace: The Toy Industry Takes Over Saturday Morning Cartoons," it said, "Eight of the 20 top-selling toys for June 1987 are toy lines which were developed simultaneously with or prior to their corresponding television specials or series. They include G.I. Joe, Alf, Transformers, Cabbage Patch Kids, Silverhawks and Pound Puppies." In essence, what seemed like relatively harmless television was criticized as just program-length commercials that children were being marketed. Children's rights groups had protested to Reagan's FCC, but the response they received from Commissioner Freda Thyden was alarming. "In true Reaganese," says the author, "Thyden says the marketplace will have to determine 'the set-up of children's programming.' Thyden says parents concerned about the over-commercialization of children's programming should be mini-regulators. 'Remove the TV from your house or keep on top of your kids,' she advises."

"Merchants of Cool"

The corporate takeover of the airwaves and Millennial mindsets did not stop there. By the time we were teenagers, Millennials had another corporate ploy to capture us as consumers. I remember a documentary shown to me in one of my sociology classes before I graduated called "Merchants of Cool," which aired on PBS. According to this documentary, released in 2001, Millennials may very well have been produced, manufactured, and sold as a commodity for corporate America to thrive at our expense. This documentary obviously did no favors for the public relations of corporations. Controversial, informative, and a wake-up call for parents everywhere, it shared a scary truth about what was happening to teenagers in America. It revealed that my generation became prey to corporations who discovered young people to be a lucrative market with incredible buying potential when adding parental "guilt money" ("I work too much, so I'm going to buy you this") and young people's own pocket money. With teenagers having a spending power of $150 billion the year the film was released, it was clear that the "corporate masters of this world" had "infiltrated teen culture, packaged it, and sold it back to teens in the form of mass entertainment media, gendered caricatures and products," as one blogger put it.

"Merchants" shared a chilling corporate secret: corporations were hiring consultants who provided "cool hunters." Their main mission was to find young people who were trendsetters on school campuses and recruit them using guerrilla tactics to get other young people to wear their corporate brands and buy their merchandise. Corporations now had access to young people directly through their peers, and analyzed data about Millennials in a way that was never done before. Through focus groups, studying the habits and behavior of Millennials, and by covertly marketing on school campuses, corporations had found a way to understand and then distort youth culture. As if in our toddler years it wasn't bad enough that we had toys in our cereal boxes, toys in our Happy Meals, deregulated commercials on television, and information that was strategically planted in our minds by Corporate America, this tactic was certainly a new low. This corporate ploy of getting in with Millennials without consent, through our own peer groups, was done in a way in which no other generation had been manipulated and commoditized.

It is hard to believe the lengths corporations went to manipulate youth consumer habits. The massive commercialization of my peers and I was no accident. One article that featured "Merchants of Cool" articulated it best when it said, "More than any generation in history, people who are young today are not free to create an authentic culture of their own. Instead, their hopes and desires are intensively studied by marketers, then amplified and sold back to them in a diabolical feedback loop."

An online magazine reflected optimistically on the end of this seemingly hopeless scenario saying, "Suddenly, people are waking up in droves from the dreamland of corporate cool. We're realizing that ever since we were little babies crawling around in front of the TV sets in our living rooms, we've been lied to, propagandized, and told incessantly, day after day, that we can find happiness through consumption. Now the fog is lifting. We're finally beginning to understand where this bogus cool has been leading us . . . This is the magic moment in which capitalist cool can stumble, and authentic cool can start bubbling back up again . . . The rest will follow."

What Happened to the Middle Class While We Were in Diapers

While we were busy being commoditized as children, our parents were slowly falling off the middle class wagon. When you look into the topic of the middle class in America, you find that the middle class has been in decline for far longer than the length of the 2008 financial crisis. The middle class has been stagnant in its wage growth since the late 1970s, and yet, it almost seems like Bill Clinton's former Labor Secretary Robert Reich is the only one that has been noticing. His documentary, *Inequality for All*, which was released late 2013, is an excellent look at this phenomenon, as well as the increase in income inequality since the late 1970s.

The middle class is perhaps the most essential segment of the economy. The demand that the middle class consumer creates is what allows companies to have a market for their products. The capital earned then goes to financing the operations of those companies. These operations, of course, include jobs; and the taxes paid on the revenue and wages of the businesses in turn finance the government. Economists will tell you the middle class consumers are the real job creators when you look at macroeconomics. Therefore, it is essential that this middle class is thriving, strong, and hopefully growing. Unfortunately, the story of the middle class in America since the late 70s is the exact opposite of this growing, healthy state. The middle class is shrinking, and inequality between workers and the executives in charge of them is growing. The real purchasing power of the median salary, when adjusted for inflation, has been declining since then.

In 1978 the average male worker was making $48,000. The average male worker in 2010 made $43,000. Meanwhile, the wages of top executives have skyrocketed. In 1978 the average chief executive officer made $390,000. In 2010, the chief executive officer's average pay had almost tripled at more than $1.1 million. What happened? Have workers become less efficient? Common sense alone (and the statistics as well) tells us that workers are now more efficient than ever. Much of this is due to advancements in technology. The technology that has helped the company become more efficient has paradoxically lowered wages for employees.

This decline in worker pay has occurred for a variety of reasons, but some of the important reasons include a reduction in the number and power of unions, globalization, a culture of corporate executive greed, and deregulation of the financial sector. The change in unions has mirrored almost identically the inequality between executives and the average worker. When these numbers are looked at in a chart it is tough to tell the two apart. Why have unions diminished in the past few decades?

That is a multifaceted evolution as well, but it certainly has not helped unions now that technology has allowed companies to cut their workforces dramatically. In *Inequality for All*, the example of Amazon. com is examined. Amazon.com is a little different in that their company is possible because of technology, and they have grown their workforce to 60,000 workers. However, the local and chain bookstores that Amazon. com has helped put out of business would have probably employed from 600,000 to 1,000,000 workers. Selling books was never a union-backed occupation, but the evolution of factory and production jobs has essentially taken the same path. The factories need fewer workers because of advances in technology; therefore, there are fewer workers. Having fewer workers has led to less power in the hands of the workers when it comes to negotiating wages.

Another factor that has shifted the employment landscape away from unions is globalization in general. The increasingly global nature of business in the modern world has put increasing pressure on companies to be competitive with the prices of their goods. A key method of becoming competitive is to cut costs—including wages. This is a large part of the motivation behind many corporations fighting the formation and power of worker's unions. It seems fair to assume that companies whose profit was being consumed by newly competitive prices in the marketplace would try to make up for it by keeping wages low. Unfortunately, corporations do not like to talk much about these types of decisions in public, but we can be reasonably confident of our analysis, nonetheless.

Entrenched Wealth

The Occupy Wall Street protests of 2011–12 were seen by the media and public as being motivated largely by rising inequality and the mortgage crisis—with a fair amount of protesting about the bailouts of banks and other financial institutions. I was there to witness these protests in person, and what most people do not understand is that these people were upset about basic fairness, as well. The bailouts and the bad mortgages that preceded the crash were unfair. However, the subject that was most lost in the noise—which is probably the most unjust of all—is the nature and existence of the tools the selfish members of the rich use to entrench their wealth.

Unlike some of the previously mentioned topics of the protests, these tools are still alive and well in America. In fact, they are worse than they were at any other time in American history.

So, what tools do the rich use to keep their wealth entrenched? Well there are quite a few, unfortunately, but the most prevalent of them all can be found on any payroll statement in America: taxes.

Payroll taxes in this country are progressive when it comes to wages. The more money you make, the more taxes you pay. So, what is unfair about that? Well, the answer lies in the fact that the vast majority of the wealthy, and nearly all of the 1%, make their money from capital gains. Capital gains are the appreciation in value of capital. A common example of capital gains is money made from the ownership of stocks.

So what exactly is the tax rate on capital gains? It is a measly 15%.

Even if that is your only source of income, you ask? Oh yeah, but let's not forget that they get to write off business expenses, as well, which takes their effective tax rate closer to 10% in many cases.

So, the wealthy have it made when it comes to taxes, but why is that? Was it just that they got lucky when the folks in D.C. created the tax code?

As anyone who has worked in politics can tell you, the only luck in politics is the kind you seem to always get when you contribute generously to the campaigns of politicians in D.C. Just to be sure though, the Wall Street folks contribute very generously to campaigns on both sides of the aisle. That way no one brings up that capital gains tax rate.

So, the tax code is rigged towards the bankers and very wealthy, but what else has their money bought them from the politicians? Well, their contributions seem to have made it a little easier to bail the big banks out during the crisis. The financial "reform" that has happened since the crash has been gutted of any real restrictions on the financial sector due to their army of lobbyists. The other interesting thing is that somehow no politicians thought of breaking up the financial institutions into smaller companies to avoid them being too big to fail—or at least creating a separation between consumer banks and investment banks—which would have prevented the crisis that occurred leading to the bail outs. This separation is what was created after the Great Depression to prevent the occurrence of another depression. Yet the Republican Party succeeded in deregulating banking again, which is what made The Great Recession possible. If that's not enough, the conservative majority on the Supreme Court has ruled that corporations (and their money) are people who are granted "free speech." This has legally been interpreted as corporations getting to give unlimited amounts of money to partisan SuperPAC's (that do not get taxed) due to the Supreme Court's decision in the case commonly referred to as Citizen's United.

The cries of Occupy Wall Street were mainly about the widening gap of income inequality between average Americans and the super wealthy in America. The latter represented the American consciousness by the bankers wheelin' and dealin' on Wall Street. Akin to the Great Depression of 1929, stocks plummeted and banks were getting away with bloody murder. A shadow banking system emerged. Former Federal Reserve Chairman Ben Bernanke defined it as, " . . . a diverse set of institutions and markets that, collectively, carry out traditional banking functions—but do so outside, or in ways only loosely linked to, the traditional system of regulated depository institutions."

American economist Paul Krugman believed shadow banking was the core of what caused the economic crisis. "As the shadow banking system expanded to rival or even surpass conventional banking in importance, politicians and government officials should have realized that they were re-creating the kind of financial vulnerability that made the Great Depression possible—and they should have responded by extending regulations and the financial safety net to cover these new institutions. Influential figures should have proclaimed a simple rule: anything that does what a bank does, anything that has to be rescued in crises the way banks are, should be regulated like a bank."

To add insult to injury, Washington was doing practically nothing to assist young Americans in their woes. In a Bill Moyers weekend reflection on the modern-day class war, he said, "The historian Plutarch warned us long ago of what happens when there is no brake on the power of great wealth to subvert the electorate . . . We don't have emperors yet, but one of our two major parties is now dominated by radicals engaged in a crusade of voter suppression aimed at the elderly, the young, minorities and the poor; while the other party, once the champion of everyday working people, has been so enfeebled by its own collaboration with the donor class that it offers only token resistance to the forces that have demoralized everyday Americans."

In Joel Kotkin's book, *The Next Hundred Years: America in 2050*, he paints a picture of what the future of America will look like for young people: "Although there is considerable mobility both up and down, wealth has been concentrated in fewer hands, with relatively fewer benefits to the working and middle class. Perhaps more disturbing, younger people with degrees lag in wage growth, accelerating inequality. This could become a long-term trend, particularly for Millennials, as they crowd into the labor market that may be far tougher than that of their baby boomer parents . . . Impediments toward upward mobility, which some studies reveal are occurring, constitute a direct threat to the national ethos. The loss of aspiration could become particularly acute among younger workers, who even before the 2008 recession were suffering diminishing economic prospects."

Millennials: America's New Poor?

So while we were still in diapers, our parents and the average American family were becoming a part of the newly shrinking middle class. We Millennials were still being taught to consume, to buy, to own, and to borrow before we could even utter our first word. Fast forward to today, and now you have young people who try to consume, try to buy, try to own, but have borrowed so much on maxed-out credit cards and student loans, that you now have: TA-DA! America's New Poor.

Personal bankruptcies. Foreclosures. Low consumer confidence and a rising cost of living. Millennials didn't have purchasing power to consume. No jobs, no money, no objects to make idols of. We didn't have a chance to pursue the American Dream. The steady decline of employment during the recession meant that our diplomas did not offer the promise of job security and financial freedom once offered to educated Americans.

Today, due to the recession, the Millennial generation is increasingly relying on lower-end financial products that were previously the tools of the entrenched and longtime poor. These tools include payday loans, pre-paid debit cards and pawn shops to name a few. Eighty-three percent of respondents to one study on Millennials said they had decent experiences with pre-paid debit cards and check-cashing services. Sixty-two percent said emergency cash services were "important."

To understand the Millennial view on finances, you must first understand a bit of the context these views were shaped in. For us, we were told that as long as we worked hard, we could go to college, and, as long as we did well in college, we could start a great career doing whatever we wanted. This fairy tale did actually seem to be coming true for us. We worked hard in school, and many of us went to college. Some did not, but many did, and some even went to institutions that were quite prestigious. For these reasons, we were quite optimistic about the next stage of the fairy tale coming true, as well. This confidence was maintained and fortified by our professors, who seemed to discuss our careers as the guaranteed formal structure involved in living out our destinies after graduation.

Unfortunately, this fairy tale came crashing down once the financial crisis got into full swing. The realization that we would be unemployed, underemployed, or employed in an undesirable position and/or industry was postponed for some of us Millennials (those lucky enough to finish school after 2007 or 2008). For me on the other hand, I graduated literally the worst year possible. The reason 2007 was so significant is that we got to see the end of what life looked like pre-recession (great job prospects, companies hiring, etc.), but then we saw all those job openings vanish with the crash of the economy just as we were sending in our resumes.

This turbulent environment has—understandably—produced some individuals with almost comical contradictions. Even the media seems to not be able to make its mind up about us. For example, *USA Today* came out with an article on April 23rd, 2012, entitled "Millennials Struggle with Financial Literacy." Meanwhile, five months later on September 28th, 2012, *The Wall Street Journal* published a piece with the title, "Who's Financially Smarter? Gen-Y Tops Boomers." Given the fact that our generation did not reinvent its relationship with money over several months in 2012, and the fact that these two publications are both usually credible news sources, how can these headlines both be true?

The answer to this riddle seems to be found by studying the data interpreted by both of these stories. *The USA Today* study looks at the fact that many Millennials perform poorly on tests of financial literacy. The story does not compare the scores of Millennials to other generation's scores at the same age, yet—even assuming the Millennials do have lower scores than previous generations—there is another fact that explains the inconsistent interpretations. Millennials are saving for retirement at a younger age than ever before in the United States. Millennials start saving for retirement, on average, at 24. Baby Boomers, on the other hand, started saving for retirement at age 35 on average. Gen X was better than the Boomers, but still procrastinated longer than Millennials, with their average age of retirement saving beginning at 28, according to *The Wall Street Journal.*

What the articles do not explain, or even acknowledge, is the reason behind us supposedly knowing less about money, yet making the financially literate decision to save for retirement at an earlier age. The pessimistic view is that pensions are not commonplace for us, and that is why we feel the need to save earlier, yet pensions weren't in the cards for most Gen X'ers either, and they waited longer than us. The Millennial experience is one in which we were never required—or, in most cases, even offered—financial literacy classes in K-12 or college. I believe we make the right decision about retirement intuitively due to the uncertainty in the job market we have seen in our early professional lives. We also have quite a few interests in life outside our careers, which makes us interested in retiring as early as possible. Finally, we are not as driven as our predecessors to make as much money as possible, at all costs. We like work-life balance, and we are willing to take a pay cut to achieve that balance. To compensate for this loss of potential income, we save more and earlier than our parents.

Another insightful piece of research done on Millennials is a study conducted by Wells Fargo that sought to understand Millennials' attitudes, behaviors and financial circumstances. I will spare you all of the numbers, but the key insights were as follows:

1. Millennials are confident in their prospects for the future and feel they are in control.
2. Student loan debt is their biggest financial concern.
3. Higher education is still the aspiration, but some question the cost/benefit.
4. They are confident in their retirement outlook, but use employer retirement plans like piggy banks.
5. They are more risk averse than Boomers when it comes to investing.
6. They are not against working with a financial advisor, however are skeptical about working with financial institutions.

When I read this study, the thing that jumped out at me was that Millennials are confident in their prospects for the future, and they feel that they are in control, despite the terrible unemployment, low wages, and lack of pensions or significant contributions from employers towards their retirement savings. When you add that to the revelation that we Millennials are taking money out of our 401K's to pay for cost-of-living expenses and debt payments, it makes you wonder why Millennials are so confident that they are in control of their futures.

I reached out to fellow young people and asked them why this might be the case. What I heard back was that Millennials are by and large confident in the future because financial security from employer wages is not our only source of confidence about the future. We are confident because we know we are capable, and we just *know* we will be okay. In fact, we are determined to be okay. Even if that means we are going to adjust our definitions of success. If we cannot be wealthy from the wages employers give us, we will be happy with the lives we live by making the things we love the priority, as opposed to money. Young people are choosing to love their lives now instead of deferring their enjoyment of life to when they retire at 65 or 70, or even 75 these days.

Short on Cash, Extended on Adolescence

Young Americans are getting into their careers later in life since the beginning of the millennium and certainly since the beginning of the recession in 2007. According to a joint study between Georgetown University Center on Education and the Workforce and The Generations Initiative, young people are now reaching the median wage income of $42,000 at the riper age of 30. This number is important because this is the measurement generally used by economists to describe when people are reaching financial independence from their families and other sources of help. This age was 26 in 1980. That is a significantly different age. In a country where we strive to improve from one year to the next and we expect to improve financially from decade to decade, this is not an encouraging number. The United States economy has been working harder and harder for more than 30 years and has actually worsened our financial situation for young people. This regression has occurred even despite increasing levels of education and fewer children and mortgages.

The other measurable reason young people are having financial trouble is related to unemployment, but it is a separate measurement. This measurement is overall employment in the age group, otherwise known as percentage of people in the workforce. While at first glance this might look the same, it is important to keep in mind that unemployment, as defined by the federal government is, "People who are jobless, looking for jobs, and available for work." However, people who are jobless, available for work, and are not looking for jobs are technically not unemployed. These people are simply not in the workforce. What has happened with young people recently is that the percentage of people in the workforce has dropped like a rock to its lowest level since 1972. Currently 29% of people age 20 to 24 are not in the workforce at all. That is almost 10% more than the rate in 2000.

Not participating in the workforce is a complicated outcome of the financial crisis, as much as other changes in the economy have been in recent years. Many young people are now choosing to go this route and forego participating in the job market. According to my research and interviews, young people are avoiding joining the labor force in a variety of ways. Many people are simply going to school because there are no jobs, or they are going back to school because they are not able to get a job that will support them with their current degree. Other Millennials have been looking for a job without success for so long they have quit. This phenomenon results in one of several possible outcomes: They move back in with their parents, they live with a significant other that supports them, or they join the growing number of young homeless people.

While researching these subjects, I came across some truly heartbreaking information. None of which has made more of an impact on me than finding out about the homelessness problem that Millennials are facing. My struggles seem truly laughable in comparison to the hellish lifestyle many of my Millennial peers have been forced into. As of today, there are more than 1.6 million homeless youth in the United States of America. Let's look at that again: there are more than 1.6 million homeless youth in the richest country on earth, the United States of America. How much did we spend on the War in Iraq again? Wasn't it like, a trillion? Why? Oh yeah, we thought that they might. . . . never mind. We have to move forward from today. Today there are well over a million homeless kids in America through no fault of their own. What should we do about that? Thankfully, our generation will eventually have the chance to answer that question.

So what else makes this generation the new poor? Well, 22 million young adults are living with their parents, and about 6 million of the group between ages 25 and 34 has moved back in with their parents (5.9 million). Oh, and out of that group 45% earn incomes below the poverty line. So, let's see: we have 45% of 5.9 million, that's 2.66 million that are poor by definition—added to the 1.6 million homeless which are obviously poor, and we are already at 4.26 million Millennials that are poor beyond even the strictest definitions.

Clearing the Record: Are Millennials Generation ME or Generation WE?

So, here we are. Millennials. Young, Educated, and Broke. And here's the kicker: anyone older than 40 years old thinks we are jerks. Heck, even some in *our* generation think we are jerks. In a rather controversial book titled, *GenerationMe: Why Today's Young Americans Are More Confident, Assertive, Entitled—and More Miserable Than Ever Before,* Dr. Jean Twenge's research finds "generational increases in self-esteem, assertiveness, self-importance, narcissism, and high expectations, based on surveys of 1.2 million young people, some dating back to the 1920s. These analyses indicated a clear cultural shift toward individualism and focusing on the self . . ."

In another Millennial social commentary featured in *Time Magazine* in May 2013, called "Generation Me, Me, Me," the article caption says, "Millennials are lazy, entitled narcissists who still live with their parents—Why they will save us all." Author Joel Stein diagnosed Millennials with the popular "snowflake syndrome"—we basically think we're all special and unique and deserve to be praised with very little achievement.

Critics came out swinging. One article, featured in *The Wire*, defended Millennials. In a notable rebuttal to the narcissism label, author Elspeth Reeve, in an article titled, "Every Every Every Generation Has Been the Me Me Me Generation," and says, "Basically, it's not that people born after 1980 are narcissists, it's that young people are narcissists, and they get over themselves as they get older. It's like doing a study of toddlers and declaring those born since 2010 are Generation Sociopath: Kids These Days Will Pull Your Hair, Pee on Walls, Throw Full Bowls of Cereal Without Even Thinking of the Consequences."

Reeve not only defends the case with counter-statistics and analysis to show that both Stein and Twenge have skewed data, but the article featured magazine covers dating all the way back to the 1960s, with writers claiming that the Baby Boomer Generation and Generation X were also coined the "Me" Generation.

Call it narcissistic, self-absorbed, entitled—whatever—the point is any label ascribed to us, whether positive or negative, was a result of Millennials doing what we were taught. Who taught us? And what were they teaching us?

There's no denying this fact: we were born with a consumer culture and advertised to identify with what we had, rather than who we were as people. As mentioned earlier, this was a pervasive part of our experience as children.

At this point, does it really matter what the "experts" are calling us? I think it matters more that we inherited the culture, the economy, and this nation. We need solutions to fix it. The Great Recession hit us in the third eye. We were forced to awaken. We will have to stretch our faith and will power further than we even know we can if we want to leave our mom and dad's house anytime in the near future.

Post-recession, the so-called "over-achievers" and "role models" of our generation are barely getting by. At 20% unemployment rates at the peak of the recession, Millennials, including my friends who went to Ivy League schools who were unemployed, were asking me—the one who was also clueless as to what to do—if I could help them find a job. It was the blind leading the blind.

Deep reflection was offered to us amidst the sorrow. We began to seek meaning instead of material wealth. Many of us resented that our generation was being used as a scapegoat for miserable decisions and ineffective leadership through no fault of our own. We found it unfair that pundits and "experts" were kicking the next generation while we were already down. We found it an ineffective way to get America back on its feet.

And if they weren't kicking us down, they certainly weren't helping us up.

In one Harvard economist's analysis of the high youth unemployment rates around the world, he said, "This could plague a generation for many years to come. Let's wait and see what happens to them in the next decade." He probably meant no harm in his analysis, but 'let's wait and see?' As if this was some spectacle or form of entertainment for other generations to sit back and watch, while the fate of the future generation continued to deteriorate right before their eyes.

More importantly, we were angry that the dialogue regarding Millennials did not come from Millennials. Examples like Occupy Wall Street shed light on the fact that we wanted meaning and truth—and we were anything but lazy and entitled. The heart and soul of the Occupy Wall Street Movement were the Millennials. The political activism of this generation helped to elect and re-elect the first black President. Millennials were the generation that set fire to the social media revolution so that the world could be more interconnected. A world in which the Arab Spring freed citizens into democracy halfway across the world using the technology our generation created. This, among many other contributions we made, was eclipsed by the media that insisted that we were "Trophy Kids" that needed constant praise and were underdeveloped adults and were coddled too much by "helicopter moms." The generalizations ascribed to us overlooked one very important fact: young people in America and across the globe were suffering.

What Do *You* Think, Millennials?

With all this daunting information, I started to ask Millennials around the country how they felt about our state of affairs since the recession. The opinions were diverse, powerful, and honest.

One Millennial agreed with the common label of "entitlement" that has plagued the generation:

It's important for Millennials to realize that, after college, the kid gloves come off, and reality will be much more harsh than what we hoped it would be. It may be time to finally develop the tougher skin that our generation lacks . . . Obviously no one can deny the effect of the recession on the economy, reduction in workforce, unemployment rise, loss of accrued wealth for many, etc. However, the constant praise and attention that Millennials have received their whole life, including participation trophies down to a comic level of getting a gold star for using the potty, Millennials tend to have an attitude that they deserve to be pat on the back and receive a gift with every completed assignment at work, have an attitude of "known self-worth" and a determination not to take crap from anyone. These attitudes are immediately and intrinsically at odds with older generations who have been dragged through the muck and came out the other side over the course of their careers. We believe that this has a great deal to do with some of the struggles that Millennials have been facing.

When a Millennial friend had seen this comment posted on my Facebook page from a fellow Millennial peer, she was outraged.

I never comment on Facebook but this angers me to no end . . . What an over generalization as far as I'm concerned. Older generations had it way easier. When Baby Boomers got out of college with a degree there were careers out there waiting for you. Homes were actually affordable and the American Dream was something attainable. Now if you have a college degree, you're lucky to still be waitressing or working at Best Buy, or doing any other job you were doing before college. The only thing that's different is now you're getting buried by student loans—paying for an education that you thought would get you a higher paying job than minimum wage. Rent is as much as a mortgage, but you'll never be able to buy a home, because no bank will lend to you. You don't make "enough" money. Yes, there are some in this generation that grew up with a sliver spoon in their mouths, but many of us did not, and we are fighting our way just as hard, if not harder, than the boomers did. Life isn't all puppies and roses for the Millennials like you think it is. And just cause I got some f**king trophy because I played a sport does not mean I feel entitled to sh*t. I've worked no less than 3 jobs since I was 18 just to get by and never complained once. So f**k off for thinking we have it so easy. I bet by the time most Boomers were 30 they had a career, a house, and probably a kid. Unfortunately the majority of our generation would be so lucky to say they accomplished all that by 30, but the opportunity just isn't there for us like it was for people back then. We're all just doing our best to make it through this life and the challenges we are facing as a country.

As I was working in Silicon Valley, these were the questions plaguing me: Are there solutions for the multiple economic problems? Will there be a shift in our priorities since a consumer culture was all that was offered to us since birth? Is there a solution to this unemployment epidemic that seems never-ending? Are the "experts" right about our generation? Were we self-involved, spoiled and entitled? Were we misunderstood? While it would take me experiencing quite a bit more in my life before I started getting answers, I did encounter more life experiences that would lead me to more questions, and finally, the solutions.

In my personal life, things were still not looking up. During that time in Silicon Valley, I received a phone call from my mother. Her health was declining. Doctors wanted her in a wheel chair at only 46 years old.

CHAPTER 2

Asia, 2008: From Medication to Meditation

"If you want to awaken all of humanity, then awaken all of yourself.
If you want to eliminate the suffering in the world, then eliminate
all that is dark and negative in yourself. Truly, the greatest gift you
have to give is that of your own self-transformation."

—**Lao Tzu**

I t was 2008. Before my 25ᵗʰ birthday, I had volunteered on two presidential primary campaigns and had fundraised for then-candidate Senator Hillary Clinton of New York.

By this point I was considered "successful" in the eyes of my peers. I made great money, had a steady job, traveled across the country 14 days out of the month, and was shaking hands with *Fortune 500* CEOs, cabinet secretaries, Hollywood celebrities and world champion athletes. I had grown an incredible network only a year out of college and rose to the top of my industry in less than 24 months.

Technology has provided so many ways for young people like me to rise through the ranks of our careers faster than conventionally possible. But that also meant I was spending more time on a computer than in front of human beings. It also meant that the majority of my phone calls were through Skype, conference calls, or through the Internet in some way. I missed human contact. I knew the buttons on my cell phone better than I knew my colleagues. Although I was happy to see relatives overseas on a computer screen, there is nothing like being in the presence of another human being. I literally only knew how my family was doing for one period of time because of their status updates on Facebook.

Despite my career success, something was still missing, and I couldn't put my finger on it.

I was a young American in the middle of, what was to become, the greatest economic collapse in U.S. history since the Great Depression.

My parents had just filed for divorce, and as my mother suffered from her autoimmune disease, lupus, her organs and physical capacity were degenerating rapidly. Because of this psychologically jarring experience, I believe it made her deeply reflect on her life and what she wanted her remaining years to look like. She decided she wanted to pull the plug on her 30-year marriage to my father. At a certain point, I didn't blame her. My parents are both such wonderful people, but I never thought they were the most compatible couple. I remember my mom and dad always saying, "We stayed together for you kids." I understood this was their time to enjoy life without the obligation of raising a family. We were adults now, and the nest was empty. They honestly did the best they could.

As my mom sought treatment, doctors saw little hope. They told her, "It's not about whether or not you'll be in a wheel chair; it's about when." She was also told she might have to go for dialysis and endure a series of chemotherapy treatments; and, to top it off, she was denied healthcare coverage by insurance companies on the grounds that she had too many "pre-existing conditions."

This state of affairs was significant for me, not only because my mom was battling a difficult disease, but because my parents had filed for divorce, we lost our homes, and my mom's health was deteriorating all within a year.

My mother was the role model in my career. To see the strongest woman I knew battle her body despite maintaining a strong mind was humbling. I witnessed the American "healthcare" system not caring for her or her health. Receiving adequate care would require her moving overseas to the Philippines—a third-world country. I knew in my gut something was very wrong with this picture. One of the most patriotic Americans I knew—my mother—was a staunch advocate for America's main street and under-served communities through our family publication and the work she did in leading a non-profit organization. She fought *Fortune 500* CEOs and Wall Street to ensure middle class families were given a seat at the table. She was a board member for watchdog organizations that ensured banks were reinvesting in communities of color and giving small businesses access to capital. She fought for the poor, the marginalized, and specifically, ethnic minorities and women her entire career. She taught me everything I knew about America's corporate world and U.S. politics. Her influence made me an active citizen in our democracy. Yet she couldn't stay in the country she served and loved dearly, because it wouldn't take care of her.

There was a time when the doctors had given her medications for virtually every organ in her body. She was given one pill to support one organ and another pill to deal with issues caused by the first pill. Soon enough, she was on 60 pills a day. It was debilitating. Everyday things became difficult for her. And the most we could do for her was to try to manage her pain.

Eventually, we had to send her to doctors in Asia that studied Eastern medicine. Their methods were gentler on the body than Western medicine and less dependent on prescription medications. Eastern medicine looked at the body as a whole—examining the interconnectedness of each tissue, cell, nerve, organ and function—trying to disrupt the body's natural system as little as possible, while alleviating her ailments.

One of the most interesting things I learned through my mom's illness was that other nations like the Philippines were not so heavily dependent on prescription drugs—specifically anti-depressants and painkillers. As a Schedule III drug, hydrocodone was the first thing American doctors offered my mom to alleviate her pain. I thought this was the norm, since so many of my peers were also offered hydrocodone for anything from a broken bone to a toothache. Unfortunately, the downside, which was discussed very little at the time, was that for an individual to continuously alleviate pain, they would have to increase the dosage over time as the body built a tolerance. And this could lead to more health problems—even death. In the United States, "One person dies every 19 minutes from prescription drug overdose." It is estimated that "80% of the world's pain pills are consumed in the United States alone" and that "prescription drug use has gone up 200% in the past ten years." What exactly, as a nation, were we trying to end here? Physical pain? Or the pain of human existence? One thing is evident: Americans do not like pain, and they think they should not have to experience much of it. This gave me pause. I realized America's New Poor might face poverty in areas beyond finances. The American Dream is on steroids these days, which means we have inherited a culture that is bankrupt of meaning beyond owning things. And a pill might seem like one of the solutions to numb us from this reality.

In an editorial written by Dr. Sanjay Gupta, the CNN chief medical correspondent, he said, "The truth is it is easier for a doctor to write a prescription than to explore other effective options to combat pain. And it is easier for patients to take those prescription pills than to search for alternatives themselves. Both those things must absolutely change."

Although the FDA has taken measures to significantly reduce pain pill abuse in America, I believe we have not gotten to the underlying reasons as to why Americans, compared to citizens of other countries, are looking for such drastic solutions to alleviate pain.

Has our culture started to embrace a quick fix to our suffering? Is there more than just physical pain that ails us? Is there a deeper truth that we are not looking at? Have we conditioned citizens to simply listen to their doctors and pharmaceutical advertisements? Have Americans not been advised to educate themselves about their own bodies?

So there I was on my way to Manila, the capital of the Philippines, to visit my mother during her lupus treatments. The Philippines had a different way of treating patients that did not allow painkillers to be a part of her regimen (as it was in the United States). My research indicates that doctors or pharmacists in the Philippines who illegally prescribe opiates could face the death penalty if convicted of unnecessarily prescribing these medications. I talked to a friend there about why their country had imposed such extreme regulations against the usage of pain pills.

He said, "If you had to nail something to the wall, would you use a sledge hammer? Very few ailments, we believe, need that strong of medicine. I believe your culture has gotten used to pill popping. We don't do that here. Also, if something is hurting us, we pray to God and ask Him to use our pain as sacrifice for those who are hurting. We are okay with suffering. Our Catholic upbringing has conditioned us to accept that it is a part of life."

Okay with suffering? That was intriguing to me. I completely understood what he meant when he said that, though. I had taken it for granted that I was okay with physical discomfort or pain in comparison to some in my generation. It is rare that you will see me pop a Tylenol or Advil for headaches or cramps or any other discomfort. I seem to just take a nap or watch a funny movie when I'm not feeling well. Because I was so traumatized by seeing my mother take a plethora of prescriptions, I have a phobia of pills. Unless absolutely necessary, I do not take many over- the-counter medications. I did find that my lack of desire for pills was actually unique among my peer group. It was well known on both high school and college campuses how to get Adderall, Ecstasy or Vicodin. Young people are taking more than just pain pills—they're taking anything you can traditionally find in a pharmacy and looking for ways to use it to their advantage. They are using extremely powerful substances to cope with normal circumstances of life.

Expectations of the Trophy Kids

The *New York Times* had published an article in April 2012 that provided personal testimonials from young people that confessed to using prescription drugs for academic advantage. These student voices shed light on using everything from stimulants, anti-depressants, pain relief and many other substances just to get work done or to bear doing it. One 16-year old student wrote, "I discovered that Adderall was everything people made it to be and more. I found a complete surge of adrenaline and ecstasy flow through my brain as I tackled factoring, science notes, and a four-page paper all in one night. Adderall is popular in my school, where it's highly competitive . . . As much as I was initially against Adderall, I cannot deny the fact that it's completely effective."

Another student shared the harmful effects of the unrealistic expectations placed on Millennials. These expectations of perfection have pushed Millennials over the edge. She said, "I'm sick of the expectation of a 'perfect' kid. The parents and educators in this article who express shock at kids using study drugs ought to look in the mirror; they are equally responsible . . . Change your unrealistic expectations or take the My Kid is an Honor Student bumper sticker off your minivan."

Academic excellence, wealth, titles, honors—these are all achievements we strive for as "Trophy Kids." Some believe these expectations have been placed on a generation in a not-so-realistic way. Because Millennials have been expected to reach certain ideals of achievement and status, some young people find a lack of value in themselves when they feel they can't measure up. The young person has been number-crunched, rated, letter-graded, and measured in ways that, maybe, our existence was not meant to be measured.

This begs the question: Have we conditioned an entire generation to pop pills as a remedy to meeting unrealistic expectations? Has the artificial rush of a high replaced the natural highs of life such as love, career accomplishments, having children, etc.? Have Millennials numbed themselves to normal, everyday experiences just to cope?

The Culture of Suffering

When my mother returned to her homeland after 25 years, I had the opportunity to observe much about the Filipino culture. I realized that being born and raised in the United States as a Filipina-American made the cultural experience very different for me. I was exposed to some cultural practices naturally through my immediate and extended family, but not so familiar with others.

A former U.S. Territory, there were remnants of America all over the place—for starters, Filipinos tend to be enamored with movies and music by American artists. Their billboard models have a more Anglo look to them. They have "Filipino spaghetti" that has hot dogs in it. Filipinos love Spam. McDonald's can be found in major parts of the city, and everywhere you go in the capital, Manila, people are speaking English. *Taglish*—a mixture of English and the national language *Tagalog*—is very commonly spoken. For example, *Tagalog* words like *keyk* are derived from our English word of *cake*.

However similar our former territory is to America, one stark contrast is this: how extremely happy many of the people are, relative to Americans. If you walk into a department store, the person helping you will just start singing. They are quick to assist you out of your car, with your luggage, or give way to you. The immediate feeling of hospitality everywhere you go makes it no surprise that some of the top industries Filipino Americans go into are hospitality and nursing.

Places like the Philippines don't have much material wealth. But what they do have, and what I've always admired, is the resilience of a people that have endured so much economic strife and inequality throughout its history—and to still apparently be happy. They have suffered tremendously as a nation through the conquest of the Spaniards, the Philippine Revolution, and the Japanese Occupation during WWII, the People Power Revolution in the late 80s, and more recently, they suffered the largest typhoon to hit land that was ever recorded. With a history like that, the Filipino people are tremendously resilient.

On top of that, as the largest Catholic nation in Asia, I believe the Catholic ethos of suffering has played a prominent role in the hearts and minds of its citizens. Their culture has managed to find purpose beyond the mortal body and painful circumstances as a "uniquely immediate and intimate experience of Jesus' presence." My grandpa once told me, "If Jesus hung on the cross for you, could you not endure this as an offering to Him to share in His sacrifice?"

And it's not just their overall culture that is happy—it's their Millennials that are ranking high on the happiness scale. In a study conducted by Viacom International Media Networks in 2013, they found Filipino Millennials to be the "least stressed and the happiest people in the world." All of the top five countries with the happiest Millennials across the globe were from the continent of Asia: 83% from the Philippines, 81% from India, 80% from China, 78% from Thailand, and 77% from Malaysia. Despite fears of unemployment, the study says

Filipinos "tend to look on the brighter side." Although 49% of Filipino Millennials believed job security would get worse, their optimism shed light on the fact that they'd rather receive minimum wage than no job at all.

Did the "culture of suffering" Filipino Millennials grew up in condition them better for the realities of pain? Was the key to have low expectations or finding gratitude for everything we have? Did the luxury and wealth of our high-tech culture offer too much instant gratification for America's young people?

Instant Gratification, Long-Term Misery

One Millennial, who grew up in a typical middle-class American suburban neighborhood, wrote in about his early encounter with drug use at the mere age of 12 years old. The rewards of drug use, as seen in teen pop-culture, music and movies, made him unaware of the long-term consequences of such potent chemicals. What started out as a rewarding, recreational dream for a popular football jock in high school turned into a full-blown nightmare. He had no idea that the society he grew up in—one promoting a hyper-masculine identity partnered with an instant gratification attitude—would nearly kill him:

> I think what my generation taught me is that I can have everything I want—now—and I can be anyone I want to be— right now. There was never any teaching from our parents, school, or the media that told Millennials that we need to work to build our self-confidence or to become a well-respected person. We were taught that we were already great people that could have anything we wanted if we put our minds to it. For that reason, I think I grew up wanting everything I liked as soon as possible. Girls, money, cars, clothes, expensive trips,

respect, and esteem from my peers were all things I wanted, and I decided I would take all of those things now. My plan was to attain everything I wanted in the most rapid and efficient way possible that would allow me to stay alive and that wouldn't make it impossible to reinvent myself later.

I can remember wanting to have the best of everything so much even in junior high school. I started my methodical pursuit of what I considered social success in 7th grade at the age of 12. I saw a kid in my biology class that was a skateboarder from up north in Santa Cruz, and he seemed to be well respected in the popular group of skateboarders that hung out with the hottest girls in school. The next day after I noticed him I made sure to sit next to him and become his friend. We bonded around our shared interest in skateboarding. I made plans to skate with him the next day.

That day we skated at a school at night and ran into some other skaters that happened to be smoking some weed in a glass pipe. He asked me, "Do you smoke?" I thought about the fact that I hadn't and had never even seen marijuana before, and I also thought about how uncool that would appear. I responded, "Oh, for sure I smoke." He bought us a bowlful from the other kids and I began my journey into using drugs as a social tool.

Within months I began selling weed myself—partially for the money—but much more so for my appearance. I understood at 12 the importance of branding myself amongst my peer group. I wanted to be seen as the crazy kid that is willing to do everything everyone else wanted to do, but was too scared to. This strategy had all the rewards I was seeking—girls, money, and most of all, respect. I now find myself wondering if people would have liked me had I not been seeking to impress so much. The fact is, I will never know.

As I went into high school my image as someone that effortlessly pushes the boundaries with no consequences was still working well, although it was getting harder. High school involved football, fist fights, cliques of tough kids and even my first friendships with gang members. The social environments I found myself in were certainly not promoted by my family. However, due to the tough-guy culture of male dominance at my high school this was the only way to be at the pinnacle of the social food chain at that time.

The other escalation in risk came with the amounts and types of drugs and alcohol I was consuming and selling. I found myself catching two court cases by the age of 16. One charge was for being a minor in possession of marijuana and another for alcohol.

Far from deterring me, the consequences I faced only helped my popularity, and I found myself taking girls to all of the dances for the calendar year at three high schools. This ended up being 12 dances a year. I graduated high school somehow attaining a 3.1 GPA while almost all of my male friends were kicked out or had to take summer school to scrape by.

Due to my SAT scores I was admitted into the University of California the following fall. The culture of college at this time (2003), and I suspect it is still the same, promoted enthusiastically intoxicants of every shape and form. My drug using and selling exploded into a situation where I was driving a heavily customized BMW with a $3,000 sound system and a $1,200 a week income that required little more than driving, weighing product and rolling joints.

I received nothing but admiration from my peers for my lifestyle and the rewards that came with it. However, along with the increases in everything else came an increase in my own consumption of drugs. When I entered into a difficult romantic relationship, my parents came close to divorcing, and my best friend died, followed closely by the deaths of four other friends, I suddenly found my body's response to drugs had changed.

I remember vividly when this occurred. I was on a trip to Peru that I took with two close guy friends. I had recently started taking anti-depressants and was drinking freely and frequently on wild nights with my friends. One morning, I had the idea to buy codeine cough syrup (an opiate) from the pharmacy in Peru. My friends agreed that this was a great idea, and we drank some. My friends enjoyed it; however they went back to drinking on subsequent evenings. Even though I had taken opiates before, my brain's response now felt different. I now wanted to take codeine more than I wanted to drink on the following several nights.

I didn't think much of it until I came across OxyContin and morphine in the same day at a party back on campus. I had a strong interest in trying them that I had never had before. I tried them, and the rest is history. I used my connections in the "other economy" and purchased $2,000 worth of OxyContin to begin selling. I told myself I was doing it because of the great 50% profit margin this drug had. That was a little lie I told myself to avoid the truth; I was addicted to OxyContin. I didn't admit that to myself until I couldn't stop taking it without getting sick.

I am in recovery now after several visits to rehab and an enormous amount of pain experienced. I paid for my strategy of instant gratification that I adopted as a 12-year-old child with the loss of my freedom from the age of 21 through 28. I wouldn't wish what I experienced on my worst enemy. The pain of opiate withdrawal and addiction dwarfs even the most painful and difficult parts of an addiction-free life. I also feel that my use of anti-depressants contributed to my brain chemistry changing. I never had dependence issues prior to taking an anti-depressant, however, months after starting them I was a full-blown addict to pain pills. If there is anything I could stress to the youth in America, it is that chemicals are never the answer to life. Rarely—and I mean extremely rarely—they may be required to preserve a suicidal person's life or enable deeply troubled people to function again. But that's their only place, in my experience.

In light of all the painful situations American Millennials were met with, because of either the consequences of what our culture promoted, or what we had to endure post-recession, there seems to be an opportunity for us to master some of the natural pain of human experience, and start naturally dealing with life's ebb and flow. For the hypercritical of our generation who think we are entitled and spoiled, suffering has actually become the norm for Gen Y post-recession. Beyond the long-term pain that comes with living in a culture of "have-it-all-now-and-consume," issues such as underemployment, chronic renting and student loan debt are the everyday burdens of the former "Trophy Kids."

Scared and Depressed Collective

Fear, whether consciously aware or not, has also played a significant role in how American Millennials were raised. We were the generation of 9–11, the War on Terrorism and the hunt for Osama Bin Laden. We are the first generation to have "a national terrorism advisory system." As teenagers, Millennials became accustomed to color-coding our fear in different shades. We have become familiar with taking off practically every piece of clothing we're wearing when traveling through airport terminals to ensure we're not a terrorist.

Eleven days after the terrorist attacks on the World Trade Center, Department of Homeland Security became a cabinet-level department. Most of us Millennials were just teenagers. The establishment of this department may have psychologically made America feel safer, but the need for Homeland Security created insecurity in a generation.

One Millennial wrote to me and said,

I was thinking about something today that directly relates to the seemingly erratic career choices that I make and how time really feels of the essence. Not only am I ambitious, but I have this additional drive that only now I've been unpacking and inspecting. Perhaps our generation's problem is partly due to entitlement, but it's also because of how we grew up partially traumatized with the wars abroad and 9–11. Those of us who seem to live on the edge and try to succeed as soon as possible might be running like mad because we feel a sense of insecurity and terror . . . Perhaps we've internalized terror and are living that fear out loud in our erratic choices—financially, emotionally, spiritually, physically and in relationships. Maybe we don't want it all right now just because we feel entitled. Maybe the truth is that we're afraid if we don't ask for what we want as soon as possible and get it, we won't get another chance tomorrow. The 9–11 thing is a known fact, but perhaps entitlement gets the brunt of the blame instead of a more terrifying truth that the media doesn't take some heat for. It was a widely and repeatedly covered subject matter for our generation's young minds, and I think we're still seeing the effects of it now.

Is she right? Have we developed a new, anxious generation in America?

An article in *NBC News* featuring a study by the National Opportunity Coalition says, "15 percent of those aged 16 to 24 have neither desk nor job." If it's not the anemic job numbers for Millennials, it's the debt, or the chronic renting they've inherited that gives them sleepless nights.

The article featured a quote from the president of Des Moines Area Community College in which he said, "A lot of times we don't want to look at data because we don't want to be depressed."

And I agree with him. So far, what has been the solution?

Prescription medication, once again, has not only been a remedy for pain for Millennials, but also for depression.

If you were to look at some of these societal issues squarely in the eye, it might "eat you alive," as one Millennial put it. An old high school friend called me and told me her experience of looking at what our generation was going through was "cannibalizing."

"Jamie, if this shit doesn't depress you. I don't know what will."

Findings from another report on *CBS News* said, "Millennials are more stressed than any other current living generation, according to a new survey conducted by the American Psychological Association and Harris Interactive."

That same report found "more Millennials reported they had depression (19 percent) compared to 14 percent of adults between 34 and 47—from "Generation X"—and 12 percent of adults between 48 to 66—"Baby Boomers"—in addition to 11 percent of seniors 67 and older."

If young people are suffering so much, why has there not been mass mobilization or an ongoing movement beyond Occupy Wall Street? I asked my co-worker. Her response was both intriguing and unforgettable: "Have you ever trashed a place? I mean, like, REALLY trashed a place? Like cooked a big meal and left the kitchen an absolute disaster? Or better yet, when you were in college, had a party suddenly set off in your dorm, and when you woke up, it was just a complete disaster? Like, mashed-potatoes-under-your-pillow disaster? Like, week-old-sushi-stuck-in-between-couch-cushions kind of disaster? Yeah, well, that's what dealing with our generation's issues is like."

Her analogy was genius. I vaguely remember most college days, but parties like that are hard to forget, so I knew exactly what she was talking about. I then asked her, "Okay then, whom do you think threw the party? Do you think they should clean it up?"

She quickly responded, "Does it really matter who threw the party? Nobody in particular 'threw the party.' Maybe the creepy guy down the hall did. The point is, no one is going to own up to it. You still have to clean it up. It's your dorm room. It's your couch. It's your pillow. You have to clean it up. Sometimes I feel like it's easier to deal with the cheap drama, Cyber Monday and the fight with my boyfriend than deal with 'cleaning up' anything for our generation. I'd rather just shut the door and go to my third job."

Mental Health in the Workplace

Millennials with three jobs or even just one job are finding it increasingly difficult to keep up with the demands of life. Stress has become the new norm for some young people, and medication has been the most prominent answer to their problems. One recent graduate of law school said this:

> I started taking antidepressants/anxiety meds when I first started working at a law firm.
>
> I went to a psychiatrist and she recommended I take an anti-depressant/anxiety med to calm myself down. It wasn't a Xanax or something that offers a temporary solution for when you have panic attacks. This medication was meant to be a long-term solution.

I took it for a year and a half, and things seemed to be fine. In the meantime, I was working at my first law firm job. My boss was harsh and rude, and although she liked me, she would constantly yell at me for things that she did wrong or for things she misread. She also once said I dressed like a whore (I never once wore a skirt mind you). People constantly asked how I could work for someone like her when she was so rude to me, our clients, and other attorneys. At that time I was just so thankful to have a job in that economy. And she was smart, so I figured it was worth it to have a job and at least learn something. At times, my anxiety got so bad I called in sick because I literally couldn't get out of bed to face her. She told me once that I was sick too often. The truth is I'm never sick—I just couldn't get out of bed because I was too anxious and I couldn't deal with her that day.

My boss was also becoming increasingly ill. She was overweight and had heart problems and went through five months where she was constantly fainting and in and out of the hospital. I stayed late for work one night and I heard this loud odd wheezy noise. I rushed into my boss's office and she was slouched in her chair, eyes wide open and staring at the ceiling. I checked for a pulse and couldn't find one. I looked down on the floor and realized she had urinated. I put my finger under her nose and didn't feel her breathing. I began to cry and smack her across the face to wake her up. She eventually did and told me not to call 911 since she was fine. I found her like this a few more times. Despite knowing she had heart disease, she did not take care of herself and she continued to eat fried and fatty foods. I began to become increasingly stressed and afraid I would find her dead when I came to work in the morning, or that she would die in front of me. I went to the Dr. and increased my dosage.

Then almost two years into my job, my boss was rushed to the hospital. I was told she was in a coma, and it was unlikely she would come out of it. I needed to come say goodbye.

Because I didn't know what was going to happen, I continued to work at the firm. There was no one else to rely on. I didn't think it was fair to our clients, so I continued to work there.

After five weeks, my boss miraculously came out of her coma. She demanded that I come to see her in the hospital. She was very short with me, told me I looked like shit (at this time I wasn't really sleeping), and proceeded to be as cruel as she once was. At this point I made the decision I was going to leave. My last two weeks were so unbearable that I ended up leaving three days early. She yelled even more and sent me mean emails from the hospital. I had finally had enough.

I have been working at my current job since August 2012 and my boss is nicer, has never once yelled at me, and the working environment is just so much more positive. And yet, I still have nightmares and anxiety in the morning. I see a psychiatrist and a therapist. At one point my anxiety meds stopped working so my psychiatrist thought she would put me on bi-polar meds to see if that helped. I ended up throwing up for three weeks straight. (I had to excuse myself twice from a deposition to throw up). I told her I couldn't be on those meds anymore. So, for the last couple months we've been experimenting with different drugs. My psychiatrist thinks that the reason I have some kind of PTSD is from working at my old place, I constantly have nightmares (about my old job and new one), I constantly am on the verge of tears at work, thinking my boss doesn't like me and waiting for her to snap on me or threaten to fire me.

I'm thankful for the experience I got at my last job, but frankly, I never saw myself being so dependent on medication like this.

Even when Millennials are in "dream" corporate jobs with decent salaries and big titles, there seems to be a solution that medication, once again, can bring if an anemic economy means fewer jobs and more candidates that can take your position. Failures not being an option, some Millennials are given pharmaceutical solutions so that they can handle the rapid pace of life that corporations require, as we see in the following testimonial:

At 27, I got the VP-level corporate recruitment treatment to join a national department store chain—unheard of for someone my age. But then I had the right network. The general pitch was that this role would help revitalize the company's outdated business model—namely, to help construct and beautify arguments in the HR department to bring in the best of the best talent from all over the country to the headquarters in Texas. Not only would this be a change of scenery, it was also a chance to negotiate my first starting bonus and a better salary. Most importantly, it was a chance to work side-by-side with executive recruiters—an investment in itself in this cruel job market.

I left a budding romantic relationship, a secure job, [and] my work-life balance, and [accepted] being away from my mom for this opportunity. The stakes were high and failure was not an option.

Success at our age can be a strange thing (and I lived this part personally). With mounting real world pressure to perform or risk being replaced by someone younger, faster and cheaper, it seems bizarre to an outsider that those of us who have "made it" aren't thrilled. Indeed, some of our parents have never seen the paychecks some of us can bring home due to a college education and a great job—this is the American Dream fulfilled, isn't it? But to some, the effect of success appears to be a negative one. As we gain promotions and are pressured by mobile technology, the pressure of being "on call," "available by email," or checking our work messages constantly is getting in the way of us separating from work when we physically leave the building. This widely accepted intrusive behavior into our private space has left us with little privacy. We walk the tightrope with the others gunning for scarcely available promotions. So, when many of us need to let off steam, we "go big." It can manifest in a multitude of ways. One way is an instantly shareable exotic trip—with a hefty price tag—to elicit envy on Facebook. Or it could show up in less glamorous, and, in some ways, unhealthy ways, like binge eating, alcohol abuse, "retail therapy," or—more alarmingly—socially accepted prescription medication. In this country, the highest levels of drug abuse stem from those that are prescribed. And this is for "successful" young adults.

After what I can only describe as a "manic sugar high" from drinking the company Kool-Aid, I quickly found myself face-to-face with the remains of 90's success–alive and well in the new company I worked for. I worked with "old corporate" people who had little intention to help move the needle and instead engaged in bureaucracy. As a millennial who wants to help make big changes, it was disheartening to work with people who wanted to maintain a status quo that works in the short run. Why rock the boat?

One day, my boss left the company with no notice, and I was bumped from one boss to the next. Trying to survive the rapid change of hands and understand the new shift in corporate direction, I became a zombie—moving from one meeting to the next with less creative juice than the day before. I needed advice desperately.

After many professional and unprofessional appeals to various executives who had little more advice than "buck up," "take up yoga," or "see a therapist," my last straw came in a private meeting with an HR executive. When I told her about my mounting stress, workload and inability to cope with daily, massive changes, she gave me the following "under the table" advice. She was concerned that my anxiety was more to do with me and less with the company as a whole, and advised I go a few floors down to see the company clinical doctor, ask for "a little something" to deal with anxiety, go to the company pharmacy and self-medicate. This advice, she continued, was something she used for herself so she knew it would help. As I felt pity that someone like her would have gone through the tough time, I was equally disgusted with her ease and authority on the subject. What has the world come to if management dissociates with their poor management skills and persuades professionals to engage in a "quick fix?"

My last Friday was dreamlike. I dropped what I was doing, packed my things, handed in my curt but direct resignation letter, and floated to my car. I had a blinding migraine— the kind I get from extended stress—and I left quietly. The HR department called for the standard exit interview, but I declined to comment. After a few attempts to reach me, they stopped calling.

Young Veterans and Post-Traumatic Stress Disorder

If we look at the numbers for depression, there's an even more depressed cohort within the Millennial generation, and those are our young veterans.

Post-Traumatic Stress Disorder (PTSD) seems to be the norm for those that are recent veterans from the conflicts in Afghanistan and Iraq. Because the average age of a service member is 25 years, you can guarantee this is disproportionately affecting young veterans.

A study from the University of Minnesota and Minneapolis VA Medical Center found that those veterans "who now attend college are far more likely to engage in risky behaviors, such as fighting, weapon carrying, and binge drinking compared with their non-veteran counterparts enrolled at a university."

A similar study done by the American Psychiatric Association 2011 Institute on Psychiatric Services (APA-IPS) discovered what happened to veterans after they returned from war. They found that it was the younger veterans who overwhelmingly received inadequate PTSD treatment for their symptoms. Dr. Jain from Researchers from the National Center for PTSD said, "Researchers were especially interested in assessing treatment of PTSD in veterans of the current conflicts in Iraq and Afghanistan, so they intentionally oversampled these patients. Fifty percent of more than 1600 patients invited to participate were veterans of Operation Iraqi Freedom and Operation Enduring Freedom."

To add insult to injury, they are more doped up on pills and are more likely to be killed by overdose than the average American.

On a *PBS News* report that aired in October 2013, they found that "the death rate from overdoses of those drugs at Veterans Affairs hospitals is twice the national average. But data shows the VA continues to prescribe increasing amounts of narcotic painkillers to many patients."

Results of a Quick-Fix Society

A controversial article written by a psychologist titled, "What's Wrong with Millennials? My psychotherapy Clients Can't Fend for Themselves," the author claims, "The big problem is not that [Millennials] think too highly of themselves. Their bigger challenge is conflict negotiation, and they often are unable to think for themselves. The over-involvement of helicopter parents prevents children from learning how to grapple with disappointments on their own . . . helicopter parenting has caused these kids to crash land."

She says these are the reasons young people are depressed. "The era of instant gratification has led to a decrease in what therapists call 'frustration tolerance.'" The inability for Millennials to deal with life's small upsets is what she claims lacks in her patients.

Critics of this article say this therapist is starting with a sample of Millennials who clearly already have problems if they are coming in to see a therapist. Secondly, they feel her criticism of Millennials has undermine the true suffering young people have gone through.

Either way, her observation of the escalation in depression—regardless of where it is derived from—is certainly confirmed by both statisticians and experts alike. As if the escalating numbers of depression weren't already problematic, the quick-fix solution has been to prescribe anti-depressants. Physicians and patients both want a quick-fix: The physician does not want to see their patient in pain and the patient no longer wants to be in pain. So whether it is painkillers or anti-depressants or both, a recipe for disaster has been cooked up for Millennials. A major problem with this is that pain is a natural part of life. It is part of the ebb and flow of human existence, so prescribing away the problem is not a solution; it's a Band-Aid. Instead of getting to the root of a problem and going inside to figure out, "Why am I depressed? Should I be depressed?" A pill has now become the solution.

If our medical doctors are trained to prescribe, rather than to look at a holistic view of what ails the patient, then, I am afraid, this trend will continue.

East Meets West with the Rise of Urban Yogis

There is good news—really good news to all this daunting information.

With extremely bad circumstances comes a sun salutation to usher in a new day.

Yoga, an ancient mental, spiritual and physical discipline which originated in India, has found itself in America's mainstream, with Millennials embracing the practice of slowing the breath, clearing the mind, and connecting with a higher source. The ancient Indian spiritual practice that started out as a trendy workout has now turned into a $10 billion industry in the United States, with 20.4 million Americans practicing yoga, according to "Yoga in America," a 2012 study.

"You've watched Sun Salutations on *Rosie O'Donnell* and *Good Morning America.* You've read the statistics everywhere from the *New York Times* to the *Tulsa World* . . . It's the most popular new feature at health and fitness clubs around the country," says *Yoga Journal.*

The benefits of yoga are numerous. In a world that promotes consumerism, yoga's tradition of mindfulness offers a counter to a "quick fix" and instant gratification culture.

Yoga Journal writer Ann Cushman says, "The longing for material-world happiness is often why people initially come to spiritual practice in general. Our spiritual cravings, to begin with, are often simplistic and even infantile. We're looking for a Santa Claus-like God to stuff our stockings. We pray for things that we want; we pray that good things will happen to us and the people we love, and we pray that bad things won't. But gradually, if we're lucky, we notice that the Santa Claus approach to spiritual practice has limitations," says Cushman.

Millennials will tell you they agree with Cushman—our illusions perpetuated more of what is wrong with America. In meeting the dragon in the lair, some Millennials are okay coming face-to-face with their suffering, and they are channeling the experience through their bodies with this ancient tradition.

"We start looking to our yoga to give us something other than perfect bodies and charmed lives: an ability to meet whatever is true in our bodies—and our lives—with grace and awareness and compassion," Cushman continues. "For us in the West, the body has become the meditation hall in which we first learn to practice the basic contemplative arts of concentration, insight, and mindfulness. *Asanas* [yoga poses] have become the tools for opening the heart to compassion and devotion; for studying the flows of breath and energy; for gently releasing the classic spiritual obstacles of greed, hatred, delusion, egoism, and attachment."

This may mean that, what started out as a pop-culture workout promoted by icons like Madonna, has become a mainstream, holistic approach to physical and mental healthcare. It is an alternative available to the next generation that was not widely accepted before. The balancing act of doing the head-stand *asana, Salamba Sirsasana,* and managing work-life balance can now be done either at home on a yoga mat, in studios that are sprawled all over the country, or even at work on your lunch break, as many *Fortune 500* companies have offered it as part of employee health and wellness programs.

Yoga and many other preventative health solutions are now becoming acceptable practices in Western medicine. As the American medical community has evolved toward more holistic approaches to countering unhealthy lifestyles, reoccurring findings conclude that there are numerous ways to improve mental and physical health, such as: exercise, eating the right foods, taking frequent breaks throughout the day to breathe, meditating, praying, reading, writing, creating something, walking in nature, petting your dog, not working too much, taking vacation, and taking a technology break—none of which require taking a pill.

Steve Jobs: Pioneer of Personal Computing or Intuitive Innovator?

In other pop culture, it is no secret that the late Steve Jobs, who revolutionized personalized computing in America, was a yogi himself. Up until his death, Jobs openly shared his spiritual practice; he had gifted each one of the guests at his funeral the *Autobiography of a Yogi* by Paramahansa Yogananda. Steve Jobs, the CEO perfectionist that he was, arranged everything—from his caterers and his guest speakers, to the artists who played at his funeral. And, of course, he planned the gift each person would receive. The gift was that of the teachings of Yogananda.

Salesforce CEO Marc Benihoff said this of the late Jobs, "If you look back at the history of Steve and that early trip to India, . . . he had this incredible realization that his intuition was his greatest gift. . . . He needed to look at the world from the inside out . . . his message was to look inside yourself and realize yourself."

The man Steve Jobs so respected (It is said that Jobs was influenced greatly by *Autobiography of a Yogi*, which was "the guide to meditation and spirituality that he had first read as a teenager, then re-read in India and had read once a year ever since") was an Indian guru who had unified teachings of Jesus Christ and Bhagavan Krishna, which Yogananda believed revealed "the complete harmony and basic oneness" of humanity that are "principles of truth and the common scientific foundation of all true religions."

Yogananda founded the Self Realization Fellowship (SRF) in Los Angeles in 1925 to spread his message of "plain living and high thinking, and to spread the spirit of brotherhood among all peoples by teaching the eternal basis of their unity: kinship with God."

Today, the SRF Lake Shrine Temple in Pacific Palisades is a spiritual sanctuary dedicated to the work and teachings of Yogananda. There, one can find a portion of the ashes of peace leader Mahatma Gandhi, where Yogananda preserved a spectacular shrine for his friend and fellow spiritual leader. Philosophies of Yogananda were akin to those of his friend Gandhi. Both promoted a practice of non-violence, and they both promoted the practice of meditation. Meditation, Yogananda believed, allowed for the self-realization of the individual.

This idea of "self-realization" is similar to the beliefs of ancient Chinese philosopher Lao Tzu, who once said, "If you want to awaken all of humanity, then awaken all of yourself. If you want to eliminate the suffering in the world, then eliminate all that is dark and negative in yourself. Truly, the greatest gift you have to give is that of your own self-transformation."

In focusing on one's connection to its higher source, self-realization leads to self-transformation. It is, as Yogananda once put it, "the knowing—in body, mind, and soul—that we are one with the omnipresence of God; that we do not have to pray that it comes to us, that we are not merely near it at all times, but that God's omnipresence is our omnipresence; and that we are just as much a part of Him now as we ever will be. All we have to do is improve our knowing."

In Yogananda's SRF Lessons for Home Study, it details that his published writings, like the ones Steve Jobs practiced, "give [Yogananda's] step-by-step instructions in the yoga techniques of meditation, concentration, and energy enhancement that he taught, including *Kriya Yoga* . . . [It teaches] the true basis of religion [which] is not belief, but intuitive experience. Intuition is the soul's power of knowing God. To know what religion is really all about, one must know God."

For such an iconic leader in entrepreneurship and technology, Steve Jobs attributed much of his talent to his practice of quieting the mind and tapping into his intuition. In Jobs' autobiography, he said, "I began to realize that an intuitive understanding and consciousness were more significant than abstract thinking and intellectual, logical analysis." He went on to say, "Intuition is a very powerful thing, more powerful than intellect, in my opinion. That's had a big impact on my work."

According to the Exploration of Consciousness Research Institute, "Intuition is that second sense that unique way of knowing something before you've been told that can help you be a better friend, escape from difficult situations or understand complex information. A heightened sense of intuition is valuable and even life-changing, and meditation can help you develop and hone your intuition."

This made me wonder, had Steve Jobs intuitively developed our favorite gadgets—the iPhone, iPad, MacBook—through a mechanism that actually had little to do with technology, and more to do with peaceful awareness? Did he self-realize his true destiny, which allowed him to design intuitively through the gift of meditation? Would this practice be widely received by entrepreneurs, future inventors, and business leaders the way Jobs had embraced it? Would it be a new way for America's young leaders to lead?

Perhaps, the best gift Steve Jobs left us was more than just revolutionary technology. He may have given us a glimpse to how his genius was cultivated by the practice of holistic health. A practice that, thankfully, is now readily available to a new generation of tech-savvy Millennials. Maybe, just maybe, a Steve Jobs will be born of the intuitive innovation the pioneer of personal computing left us in his legacy. And more importantly, maybe a new generation of innovative Millennials will revert to more healthy solutions than the ones most commonly utilized in today's society.

CHAPTER 3

Europe, 2009:
Global Millennials

"Not all who wander are lost."

—J. R. R. Tolkien

"I'm moving to Barcelona."

"What?" I replied in utter shock.

"I was hired by a software development company. I have a work visa, and I'll be out there for at least a year."

I got goose bumps. That kind of adventure excited me.

I have always been googly-eyed about risk-taking men, and I felt this attraction start to come on. He was my old college friend, Eric, whom I had met my first semester in college at UC Santa Cruz. He had come back into my life through a random Facebook status update I came across on my newsfeed. He posted that he was in Berkeley for the evening. This was convenient because I was living in Oakland at the time. I had just broken up with my college boyfriend, so I was certainly eager to get out of the house and shake off my post-breakup blues. I also was just recovering from dealing with the loss of my home, my mother's recent diagnosis with lupus and my parents splitting up. Anything to distract me from my own personal Armageddon was a priority on my list of things to do that day.

I met him at the BART station before dinner, and we headed to Elephant Bar for a meal. As he got into the car, I felt like an old soul from the past had walked back into my life from a previous lifetime. I recognized something about him far more than his physical appearance. I recognized his energy. It fit like a puzzle piece with mine.

We hadn't seen each other in nearly two years. And even when we did see each other on campus, we were more like acquaintances. I didn't know that night I would be building a movement and a business with someone I had such an understated relationship with in the past.

Eric was your classic Millennial, but he was ahead of the curve among our peer group in the way he thought. He carried himself like a typical, young, West Coast Millennial: California-cool, trendy, laid back and loved to party. Behind the veneer, though, his cool, calm, collected nature married with a very casual demeanor would not have people think he was as perceptive as he was; sharp as a nail, and socially aware of his environment at all times. He had experience working for high-level boutique consulting firms with clients like Microsoft, but you would have never known it, because his priority was always making people feel comfortable around him. His background in strategy and thought leadership intrigued me because he was known more as the guy who threw parties on campus—not the intellectual academic that he turned out to be.

He was taking this assignment in Barcelona to provide marketing consulting, and it was right up the alley of a "dream job" for a Millennial.

According to a study conducted by Deloitte and Touche regarding the leadership styles of Millennials, it found that "Millennials demand career growth,—and lots of it . . . They want to move rapidly, they want global assignments; they are willing to embark on short term assignments, and they want development."

Globalization, the interdependence of national economies, and the Internet have all played a significant role in the way Millennials around the world operate. In a study done by JWT Intelligence called "Meet the BRIC Millennials," they found, "Millennials are regarded as the first global generation, with more overlapping values and shared experiences than any before them."

JWT Intelligence surveyed and examined different aspects of global Millennials. From personal finances to changing gender roles, social good and stress, they measured that Millennials all over the world seem to have more similarities than differences.

That is why Eric's assignment excited me. The first thing I wanted to do after graduating was travel the world and meet other young people and engage in the global economy. He had already booked his ticket and found an opportunity to work abroad; I felt a sense of urgency in booking my plane ticket and following right behind him.

That night when we connected on social media, surprisingly, turned into a very deep and engaging evening—deeper than most first dates turn out to be. After talking over dinner regarding topics like the economy, our hopes for our generation and our ambitious agendas, he leaned in and said, "You have the most beautiful mind of any woman I've ever met."

Then he kissed me.

I felt a bittersweet knot in my stomach come on. I felt my heart open up through my mind like it never did before, but this guy was leaving for a year to work abroad. If this progressed, we wouldn't have much of a long-term commitment available.

"I want to visit you in Spain," I said.

"Yes, come visit," he responded.

We both knew that night of romance would only be that night. The distance would not make a relationship possible.

Eric left for Spain three weeks later. I called the airline immediately after his departure and said, "What's the best rate I can get for November? I'd like to have a stop-over in Paris then have my final destination Barcelona."

Paris & Barcelona: Party of One

"I have some bad news," he reluctantly said. "My work screwed up my visa, and I have to leave in the next couple of days, or else I won't be able to come back to the EU if I overstay."

I quickly responded, "But I'm coming in a few weeks. I already booked my flight and hotel."

"I'm so sorry, Jamie. Like I said, the paperwork for my work visa had some errors, and the only way I can remedy the situation is if I go to the Embassy of Spain in the United States. I'm coming home early."

At first I was going to cancel my reservations. But then I thought, "Hmmm . . . this might be an opportunity for me to create my own adventure. I always wanted to see the Eiffel Tower. And besides, when else will I have the opportunity to travel? Once I have a career, I'll probably be glued to a desk and cubicle."

So, I embarked on the journey alone. I packed my bags and headed for Paris. I was not the least bit scared. If anything, I was excited. I could feel my independence. I could do what I wanted, eat what I wanted and go wherever I wanted without having to worry about other people. And Barcelona! I have always had an appreciation for beautiful architecture, so the opportunity to see Antoni Gaudi's work was a once in a lifetime experience I was willing to take.

After the excitement I thought, "Well, what pictures will I have if I travel alone? Selfies in front of the Eiffel Tower? Not a chance!"

So, I went on Craigslist, and I looked under "Paris Photographers." There, an ad read: "Freelance professional photographer, available for assignment. Portfolio provided in the link below. Message me for rates."

I emailed the photographer:

Hello,

My name is Jamie. I am traveling from the United States. I would like a private photo session if you are available. I can offer 200 Euro.

The photographer responded:

Hi, Jamie:

My name is Adam Von Mack. I am a fashion photographer in Paris. May I ask what these photos are for?

My response:

This is a very special time in my life. I've had a lot of life changes recently, and I want someone to capture this moment so I can remember it. I hope you are agreeable to my budget. That's the most I can offer. I saw your portfolio, and I can see your work is worth more than 200 Euro, but I hope you accept my offer.

—Jamie

Adam agreed to photograph me—but only for one hour. I could tell by the quality of the photos in his portfolio that 200 Euro was almost an insult. He had photographed for *Elle*, *Cosmopolitan* and for fashion magazines in Hong Kong. I wasn't his usual client, but I was grateful he took me up on the offer.

A Photo Shoot Looking through a Different Lens

I went to the Eiffel Tower, Sacre Coeur, Arc de Triomphe, Champs Elysees, the Louvre and Notre Dame—all in two days. I started to have a serious love affair with the city. It was everything I heard about and more. Upon arrival, my cab driver picked me up in a Mercedes—because almost all their cabs are Mercedes Benz's or Volkswagens—and he was so kind to welcome me to the city. My hotel room was princess pink. I heard that Parisians didn't care much for Americans, but Parisians were nothing but kind to me my entire stay. There was an air of class and grace in their mannerisms that I appreciated, and the food was delicious. I even watched can-can girls at the Moulin Rouge and met tourists from all over the world in one van ride to our show.

I decided to go to an internet cafe to update all my friends and family on Facebook that I was alright.

First thing I wrote:

Life is f**king awesome (mom if you're reading, sorry; there's nothing else to describe it)!

As I settled in on my third day in Paris, I finally met my photographer. He waited in the lobby of my hotel as I was getting ready. As I came down the stairs, I greeted him with a handshake and said, "Nice to meet you, Adam. Thank you for agreeing to do this."

To be completely honest, it probably wasn't the safest thing in the world to arrange a meet-up with a complete stranger when traveling alone. Thankfully, he wasn't an axe murder. I had a twenty-four-year-old's mentality of being overly trusting, but all in all, the risk was worth it, because the two days with Adam provided such insight to the world around me and to what was happening to young people across the globe. I found someone to share our mutual experience of pain with in a photo shoot, of all places. I had found a friend and confidant in the two days that I learned about Adam and his quest to be a successful, young Parisian fashion photographer in a very crowded industry.

By 2009, the economy was left crippled in a frenzy of Wall Street greed and deregulation from Washington, D.C. The global financial meltdown was like a falling house of cards on citizens everywhere. Despite this, Adam moved from Germany to Paris to start his own fashion photography business. His spirit of entrepreneurship was unstoppable. His British girlfriend, who grew up in Hong Kong, worked for a model agency. He photographed for models, and she booked them. Their complimentary jobs, as well as their well-traveled background, made them a perfect pair in the industry.

The minute he and I started talking on our way to the Eiffel Tower where my pictures were to be taken, we had so much to discuss. A one-hour photo shoot turned into two days with him and his lovely girlfriend, Gillian. We discussed more than photography. We discussed his desire for the European version of the "American Dream" in Paris, his desire to have his own business, his hopes for the future, and what growing up in

Europe was like. I asked him if he and Gillian were able to weather the financial storm in France, and I inquired about what his experience as a business owner was during the financial meltdown. Having originally being born in Hungary, he explained that he moved from his current hometown of Hamburg, Germany, to Paris to pursue his dream as a starving artist in an economy that did not favor his industry or his age.

If one didn't know he was European, it sounded very similar to the same dreams young Americans have. I started to see parallels between his Parisian dream and the dreams of young Americans being dashed by a lack of opportunities. I was eager to learn more. As we took photo after photo, he detailed his arrival in Paris with such ease. I had certainly found a new friend. His unforgettable story went something like this:

> You know what Paris is known for, Jamie. It's stereotypically the city of romance, fine arts and fashion. My image of Paris was from all the movies and pictures I saw: people munching on croissants, delicious cheese, and lovely French women with style walking the streets. I dreamt of long strolls along the Seine and picturesque romanticism of the Marais; I wanted it to one day be my home.
>
> Having been born in Hungary, where one finds rather limited possibilities to become one of the world's "famous fashion photographers," I decided to gather some money and go to Paris where I was convinced the magic would happen. I envisioned a French version of the once famous American Dream, where everything is possible. I immediately bought a bus ticket from Budapest to Paris and set off to the French capital with my then soon-to-be-ex-girlfriend waving goodbye.
>
> After a rather lengthy 16-hour bus ride, I arrived in Paris to an international bus station in the eastern part of the city. I went to my friend's place that was able to assist me with

accommodations for the first few days while I sorted out my new life in France.

In the days that followed, I walked around my new town and explored as much as I could. I was not typical in my ventures, as I did not go seek the famous tourist spots Paris is known for; Rather, I purposely wanted to get lost in the old streets first, and discovered the many amazing treasures that I found along the way. The city was spectacular the first few days. The French architecture, the cafes, and the restaurants stunned me. I longingly stared from outside the windows since I could not afford much in the city, but what I saw inside was no less impressive than expected.

After exploring the alleys and small hidden streets, I found myself standing under the giant structure of The Eiffel Tower. This was certainly the highlight of my experience. [For me,] a natural history buff, it was more than just a pile of neatly arranged iron that is pleasing to the eye. It was a part of history I cherished. All the other amazing parts of the city made me fall in love with the place immediately.

However, soon after the honeymoon phase was over, living there and visiting Paris became two very different experiences that I immediately became aware of.

That past dream I had of walking on the Seine? Well, I realized after living there that the long walks along the Seine were rather dangerous. And if not dangerous, then you're in for a different kind of romantic walk. I guess you could enjoy the fragrance of ammonia from urine on your 'romantic' walk. Better yet, the rats around the canal can add to the charm, and the constant noise of ambulance sirens could replace the violins in your dream. Hardly picturesque if trying to enjoy a sunset during a stroll in the city!

As a young and ambitious photographer, I pursued every possibility I had to get my foot in the door of the Parisian fashion industry. I caught a bit of luck, as I made it into fashion houses, well-established photography agencies, studios and magazine publishing houses. I did receive scowls every now and then from receptionists who would roll their eyes at my naivety of the Parisian lifestyle and mentality. They were less than impressed by my well-polished English knowledge and my young age. My country of origin didn't help me fit in either, but that didn't stop me.

I had been running my rounds in Paris for several months, eventually gaining the trust of some model agencies to shoot test photos for their model portfolios. This felt like a giant achievement after having so many doors closed at the many fashion houses I had visited. The biggest mistake I made was, of course, going to Paris without learning to speak French. The only few terms I knew my first months there were "Omelette du fromage" and "Huh?"

In Paris, one must speak French—it has been a significant part of the Parisian culture, and I guarantee it will never change. If you don't "parlais" in French, then you can expect nothing more than a short and cruel "non" to whatever you want. So this was lesson two for the clueless Eastern-European fellow.

Unfortunately things did not go as planned timing-wise. I did not have my career goals sorted out in time before I started to run out of resources. And in Paris, just like anywhere else, unexpected circumstances can get so rough that the money in your wallet becomes equal to the value of a half-eaten, week-old croissant. Accommodations of any kind in Paris are extremely expensive and definitely not something I was truly ready for. This coupled with unreliable sources of money from the small shoots I was doing, late payments or stiffed payments from clients soon resulted in me running out of money—even a roof over my head at one point. As romantic as Paris can be, the nights were not so pleasing on the streets of Gare du Nord. I would sleep with one eye open, clutching my camera bag, which was literally the only thing I owned. There are a great many shady and dangerous folks roaming the streets at night in Paris. While many tourists enjoy the parties, restaurants, the fantastic opera or just simply the warmth of a hotel, the city showed me a less than hospitable version of itself.

Luckily, I tend to be about a head taller and bigger than most people in Paris, so I never ran into any trouble. Still, it didn't make the experience any easier. After a few days of drinking tap water and eating sugar cubes, I eventually received some projects and found my way again.

During this entire Paris experience, I still have not reached what I hoped for in the French capital. For many years it was a struggle—and it still is. Just like the many others who are bold enough to venture into the world of fashion, and especially as a business owner with no particular support during this economy, it has been difficult. But on the other hand, I have learned many things, which I can be only thankful to Paris for. Paris is still a very beautiful city, but it is always difficult for me to pass the Gare du Nord or the places I slept when I was homeless, because it reminds me of a painful time. Those days in Paris made me humble and helped me never to take anything for granted. I believe it even affected the way I see things through my camera lens today as a photographer. Yes, very much, in fact.

Since then, I have had to live in more than a dozen European countries to seek other economic opportunities. I still go back to Paris regularly, as the city is still highly influential on my business, but more importantly it is an emotional experience for me. After all, it is still the most romantic place in the world, and I still find my heart there.

Adam's story moved me in ways I didn't expect. I came to learn that the Millennial struggle of finding a dream that didn't quite pan out because of economic situations was universally shared. He went on to tell me that this issue was not only for those who immigrate to France. Adam's immigrant experience seemed to be shared by those born and raised in France, as well. In an article titled, "What Millions of Young People in France Really Think," it shared a story about a photo shoot concept that included young French people holding signs with one-liners providing insight on what their most pressing concerns as citizens were. And what was the shared theme in their concerns? Not surprising: the rising cost of living and the shortage of jobs in their own country.

The article details a conversation with 21-year-old Patrick DuFour who was a student and barman who was "finding it stringently difficult to balance his studies and meet the rising cost of his rental apartment, which recently increased by 30 percent." DuFour says this is due to the fact that rent has increased by 200 Euros. "Add to that the cost of utilities, energy and food," DuFour continued, "and it is nearly impossible for me to continue school, while at the same time working to meet living expenses."

Indignados: The Angry, Jobless Generation

After my trip to Paris, I stayed in Barcelona for a few days. Gaudi's hand in the architecture of the city blew my mind. The delicious food as I walked the streets of Las Ramblas, the open markets and lively nightlife made me never want to leave. However, America was calling me back to her shores. The state of affairs in Spain was becoming more unstable. In the five years that followed after my trip, a cascading series of demonstrations occurred across Europe—with Spain being a central player in the Millennial uprising.

By 2011, protests erupted in Spain and Greece that were characterized by young, angry citizens. Because of high unemployment rates, austerity measures and debt-heavy European countries, the series of economic woes left little hope for young people. Spanish university students mobbed Madrid's central square, Puerto Del Sol. It became what NPR called "the epicenter of a new and unexpected movement of those who call themselves the *indignados*—the angry ones. Chanting, 'They do not represent us,' protesters denounce a political class they say has ignored the plight of the younger generation."

Spain, which was once envied for its economy and standard of living, by 2013, was dealing with a 26 percent unemployment rate and 56 percent unemployment for those 24 and younger.

In a *New York Times* article published in November 2013 titled, "Young and Educated in Europe, but Desperate for Jobs," it highlighted how dire the situation was in Europe. "Youth unemployment has climbed to staggering levels in many countries: in September, 56 percent in Spain for those 24 and younger, 57 percent in Greece, 40 percent in Italy, 37 percent in Portugal and 28 percent in Ireland. For people 25 to 30, the rates are half to two-thirds as high and rising," the author detailed.

Beyond that, it matter-of-factly noted, "There are no signs that European economies, still barely emerging from recession, are about to generate the jobs necessary to bring those Europeans into the work force soon, perhaps in their lifetimes."

An *NBC News* report regarding the same topic interviewed a young lady named Barbara Victoria Palomares-Romero who lives with her parents in a Southern Madrid working-class neighborhood. The 22-year old said, "Our generation is a lost cause because they don't let us work . . . Even though I'm 22, my resume is two pages long. And that's because I have done everything . . . I have done everything and can't find anything."

The report further stated daunting statistics, once again, leaving very little hope. For European Millennials, "Relief could be years away," the report stated. "The International Monetary Fund (IMF) recently forecast that the country would be stuck with 25%-plus general unemployment for another five years. This is one of the highest rates in the entire industrialized world."

American Dream 2.0: Dreaming with the World

After listening to all this doom and gloom, it was hard for me not to get choked up. I have a confession to make: That night, I cried for humanity. I don't blame people for wanting to go numb to the happenings of the world, and to not look at these numbers or read the newspaper. They don't want to feel like I did. I believe if one were to squarely look at the state of affairs of this world in the eye, it would spiral any normal human being into depression.

I was choked up that night thinking of all the people that have suffered through inefficient government, the scarcity of jobs and money, and the lack of hope they felt in their circumstances. My heart felt so much compassion for those that are affected by these poorly constructed, man-made decisions.

I knew intuitively that night that I didn't just wake up so I could feel fear and anxiety. I woke up because I wanted to give back to my country and to the world. I desperately wanted to find a solution. I wanted to finally look at the truth without dwelling on it. I wanted to get past it immobilizing me and, instead, channel the worry into action. I knew if I didn't figure out the formula to getting past all this, there was no way I could send the message I soon found to be core to my soul's mission. And the message was this: If America's youth can get it together, we can do what our country has always been good at doing, which is to support each other in innovating new solutions to problems, which in turn creates advances in technology and supports other nations in their pursuit of happiness and relative comfort. I wanted to see a different kind of diplomacy that didn't involve supporting other nations with just military support or weapons; I wanted to see diplomacy that promoted the economic freedom of citizens all over the world.

That night, I recalled Adam's immigrant story to Paris. His desire to live his European version of the "American Dream" was seared in my mind that evening. That's when one very important fact dawned on me: When American citizens dream, we dream not only for our country, but we have dreams for the *world*.

And I'm not talking about the superficial interpretation of the American Dream that is barely accessible to this generation. I'm talking about an American Dream that is cognizant of the interconnectedness of the world, an American Dream that looks to be globally responsible and that understands how small the world has become through technology. This makes it even more important that we carry out our responsibility as global citizens to achieve our nation's happiness without forgetting our brothers and sisters abroad. In our domestic policies, our commerce, our education, and in our personal lives, I believe the new American Dream is about having a global vision of peace and prosperity for the world.

So, if we are to dream this new dream for the world, how do we get past all the news articles and bullsh*t negativity that paralyzes us? I've noticed a great deal of people shut off the valve to their heart that connects them to this vision. They get to hide from negative emotions using this empathy-numbing strategy, but they never get to fully feel what life has to offer when you do feel your emotions.

If you are experiencing this, do you feel despair then walk away from it? Do you claim apathy thinking you can do nothing with this despair but feel hopeless? What other point do we have on this planet, if not for helping and promoting the life, liberty, and pursuit of happiness for our neighbor, our country, and everyone in the world? What other purpose do we have here other than walking the journey in overcoming life's challenges and emerging victorious? What else is the journey about?

I ask these questions, but I don't expect all the same answers. However one chooses to pursue peace in their lives is entirely up to them. For me, personally, what brings me happiness is finding truth despite the despair. And I'm not talking about the emotion of happiness; I'm talking about the happiness that *peace* brings. The emotion of happiness is fleeting, but the feeling of peace is sustainable. I seek the latter. And what brings me the latter is my knowing I have been a conduit to peace. The world is my village. In whatever capacity I can help to make sure everyone in the village has a filled tummy, adequate care, and equal opportunity to share in the sustained peace, I will do it.

In this global village, America has often been a beacon of hope amidst the dark night. Our symbolism as a group of citizens that believes in the freedom and independence of the human spirit to flourish has never died, despite the current state of affairs or the statistics that make it look like there is no way out. Beneath the veil of animosity and divisiveness of our national politics, the heart of America is strong. This is why my pride in being an American citizen is so fervent. In my pride as a citizen, I find it my duty to participate fully in the political system to bring these opportunities of peace to the world village. However, because America is going through such a tumultuous time, my hope—occasionally—has waned. During one of these moments, there came a time when I knew it was essential to turn a new page in my consciousness and prove that the numbers were not the entire story of our generation.

Italy Speaks: The Pope Who Gave Us Hope

After reading about the unemployment challenges, I started looking for *some kind* of information that could give me hope. I found no reason to sit in the "doom and gloom" of economist projections. I didn't want to be naive about the state of affairs for young people globally; but I also didn't want to buy into the naysayers that don't believe we Millennials have what it takes to turn this ship around. I knew from the hundreds of Millennials I had encountered in my own travels that it was impossible that they didn't have what it took to change the trajectory of the world. That "can-do" spirit was shared in America, in Asia, and in Europe—I felt the narrative from media was a one-sided story.

The next morning, I stumbled across an article in an Italian publication, *La Repubblica*. It featured an interview with the newly appointed Pope Francis. The interview lit up my mind and my spirit. I finally understood why so many people were having a difficult time addressing these issues. The Pope said:

> The most serious of the evils that afflict the world these days are youth unemployment and the loneliness of the old. The old need care and companionship; the young need work and hope but have neither one nor the other, and the problem is they don't even look for them anymore. They have been crushed by the present. You tell me: can you live crushed under the weight of the present? Without a memory of the past and without the desire to look ahead to the future by building something, a future, a family? Can you go on like this? This, to me, is the most urgent problem that the Church is facing.

I understood it. I felt the compassion warm my heart. *They are crushed under the weight of the present*, as the Pope said.

This Pope brought me genuine hope, for my country and for the world. When the Pope spoke of these two groups and clearly understood their suffering, I was moved. To have the church speak in a way that connects two of the most unspoken topics in the national discourse, with a clear understanding of the pain of this generation? I never thought I'd see the day. According to a report by NPR, "One-fifth of Americans are religiously unaffiliated—higher than at any time in recent U.S. history—and those younger than 30 especially seem to be drifting from organized religion. A third of young Americans say they don't belong to any religion." In a time when young people are "losing their religion," it was so wonderful to see a world leader mentioning the woes of young people everywhere, and to acknowledge the needs of the old, too. The intergenerational dialogue was finally on a credible platform, and Pope Francis ignited a fire that resonated with my heart and dreams for the world.

I, apparently, was not the only young person moved. In an article by the *New York Post* titled, "Just how cool is the Pope? Wayward Millennials flock to church," it talks about how the Pope took the first "papal selfie" and has made "Catholicism cool in 2013."

"There's a new spirit in the church right now. I'm hearing that young adults love Pope Francis. After all," the article continues, "he's taking selfies with them."

On December 11, 2013, *Time Magazine* named Pope Francis "Person of the Year." His humility, his compassion, and his advocacy against income inequality around the world, and the fact that he was once a bouncer in his younger years, have excited global Millennials.

On top of that, he shares something in common with singer Frank Ocean: MTV's college channel named Pope Francis Man of the Year, with singer Lorde taking the Woman of the Year.

Obama's Inauguration and the Affordable Care Act

As all these global issues were surfacing, back home in the United States I was invited to attend President Obama's inauguration in 2009. This was a pivotal time in American politics. America was caught between two very polarizing energies: that of the newly formed Tea Party movement which was anti-government in its platform and an energized liberal bandwagon in D.C. with our country's first black president sworn into office. Despite political ideology, this was truly a historic moment for our country.

Within the first six months of President Obama's first term, as a Democratic activist in the national Asian American business community, I was invited to town halls, press tours with the Administration, the First Lady's community initiatives, and some of the first community meetings that set the stage for the Affordable Care Act—President Obama's signature law that attempts to fix the healthcare system in America. I was shaking hands with everyone from Michelle Obama to Jesse Jackson and Al Sharpton. I saw the President at least three times during that period, and was invited to some of the high-level roundtables that national community leaders were attending. I was beyond honored, but noticed something I hadn't noticed before. I was now within a group of people that helped to advise the President and his cabinet on ways to fix our country's broken system, but young, minority women were a rarity at these meetings. Most of the people invited were middle-aged and talking about issues that affected Baby Boomers. They were not discussing the high-unemployment rates, the youth that were uninsured, or the concerns of Millennials.

Although I was invited to talk about small business and contracting, since those were my technical areas of expertise, my heart really wanted to speak on behalf of my generation. When anyone from the Administration would introduce me, they would highlight my business background. But anytime I had the opportunity to ask questions or speak off the cuff about the particular issue they were addressing, I always spoke as a young person.

One specific roundtable in May of 2009 was a White House discussion with Nancy Ann De Parle, who was President Obama's healthcare czar. Larry Summers, Director of the National Economic

Council, was also present, and I was invited among a total of about twenty leaders nationally. I noticed I was the only young person at the table again.

I was disappointed with the fact that universal healthcare was not only being watered down through private negotiations between the two political parties, but that young people did not have a voice at the table. Obama had created a clause that said young people could stay on their parent's insurance until the age of 26. But what happens to those who 1) have parents who don't have insurance and 2) because of the wide age-range of people hit by the recession, are over 26 and are still under-employed with no benefits?

Many of the young people I encountered were either going to school and working low-paying entry-level positions to keep up with their rising living costs, or simply didn't qualify for most government programs because they made "too much" to be categorized as poverty level, and too little to truly pay for healthcare consistently.

At this point, I wanted to do something. I decided to start a company with Eric that was a social entrepreneurship venture. We would provide access to the federal government for underserved small businesses and provide business development for the products and services of minority- and women-owned businesses. We also started a non-profit, GenerationDrive, which would mobilize young people all over the country to address these global Millennial issues of high unemployment, lack of financial literacy, and lack of training in entrepreneurship.

This is when my next journey took me back to D.C., and this time, I jumped into the lion's den of politics for two years.

The Middle East: Rise of the Arab Spring
Meanwhile, in the Middle East, the Arab Spring, a set of revolutionary demonstrations and uprisings throughout the region, was taking place the year following my Europe trip. Dissatisfied with their

political leadership, the Arab world had an uprising that their national governments were not prepared for. In 2010, the overthrow of Egyptian dictator Hosni Mubarak played a signature role in the movement, with Millennials leading the way. Taking to the Twittersphere and social media, the mark of young people on a coup d'état spoke volumes to the world of what a force young people had become.

Two years after the Arab Spring in 2012, young leaders like Malala Yousafzai were coming into the spotlight. A young Pakistani who lived in a village where education was banned by the Taliban, she provided a voice through an anonymous BBC blog for women and girls in her country advocating for every Pakistani citizen's right to education. Malala survived an assassination attempt when she was shot for advocating for women and education. Brave Millennials were popping up all over the world, and Malala was no exception. She was shot by a fundamentalist militant with an AK-47 assault rifle, yet she survived and has continued her fight with renewed passion.

In her book, *I am Malala*, she so poignantly states, "Let us pick up our books and our pens, they are the most powerful weapons . . . I raise up my voice—not so I can shout, but so that those without a voice can be heard . . . We cannot succeed when half of us are held back."

Her commitment to education and her non-violent approach to the Taliban, despite their attempt to assassinate her, moved everyone from the United Nations to President Obama—who invited Malala to the Oval Office to honor her bravery.

Washington, D.C., 2010: The Crisis of Student Loan Debt and Education in America

"Education is the most powerful weapon which you can use to change the world."

—Nelson Mandela

I t's 5:35 in the evening, and I inhale the muggy air as I pace to the next Metro Station to come home from work. In my sleek pinstriped skirt, crisp white button-up top and red four-inch stiletto heels, I catch the train just in time before the door closes. I stand, grasping the pole and catching my breath. The background noise fades in and out as I listen for the conductor to call my stop. As I exit the Metro Station I hear chants across the street from the station, outside of my English basement apartment on Capitol Hill.

"Fire Pelosi! We want her out! Obama is the modern day Hitler!"

It was 2010, and two months since I had officially become a D.C. resident. Eric and I had opened our business and started our non-profit, GenerationDrive. Also at this time, the Obama Administration had appointed Eric's dad Assistant Secretary for Postsecondary Education. This development gave Eric and I front row seats in watching the whirlwind of Washington D.C.'s battle on Capitol Hill. A new faction of the Republican Party had emerged, and they were running in key districts to help Republicans win back the House of Representatives.

ABC News reported in 2010, "By the end of primary season this year, it was clear the Tea Party had emerged as a full-fledged political force."

And the Tea Party's darling? None other than the woman news anchors called "Mama Grizzly:" Sarah Palin. And maybe that's why the Tea Party was so successful in their efforts. They had a woman leading the charge for change. *ABC News* went so far as to call 2010 "Sarah Palin's America." We saw her everywhere. From her reality TV show to her daughter's debut on "Dancing with the Stars." There is no question that the media was eating out of the honey jar with Mama Grizzly.

The same report continued: "Through her political action committee, SarahPAC, which raised millions this year, her Facebook and Twitter pages, her public speeches, candidate endorsements and television appearances, Palin managed to insert herself into the thick of the electoral politics and command more media attention than perhaps any other Republican political figure."

Education: The Problem or the Solution?
The contentious divide in D.C., fueled by the extreme ideologies of the Tea Party, was not making the majority of Americans happy. In June of 2010, 6 out of 10 Americans in the Gallup polls conducted said, "Most

members of Congress do not deserve re-election." These are the highest totals in Gallup's history of asking this question.

The data from that same Gallup poll explained that the main reason Americans did not believe members of Congress should be re-elected was that they believed they were "doing a bad job or just are not doing their job, period." The second most prevalent response was that Americans believed members were making decisions "based on inappropriate or ineffective criteria," which included the perception that elected officials were self-interested, playing partisan politics or basing decisions on their special interests.

The overall perception?

"They are not working for all Americans and the interest of the entire country" according to the poll.

Millennials were no exception to the lack of faith Americans were feeling in the system. This certainly was not the time for Washington to be ineffective; however, they were. In a *Time* magazine article titled, "Student Loans Are Becoming a Drag on the U.S. Economy," it said, "student loans now top $1 trillion, and 81% of the most burdened borrowers—those with more than $40,000 of student debt—have private loans with interest rates of 8% or higher, according to the Consumer Financial Protection Bureau. Unlike federal student loans, private loans not only cost more, they offer less repayment flexibility and typically cannot be discharged in bankruptcy. Almost all student debt is difficult, if not impossible, to refinance—sticking borrowers with high rates in a low-rate environment and adding to the economic drag."

To add insult to injury, at a time when financial aid for students was most needed amidst the economic recession, the Tea Party Republicans were trying to do away with two critical elements of the federal government: 1) They were trying to reduce funding of the Pell Grant Program, which they successfully did, by cutting summer Pell Grants, and 2) They proposed completely eliminating the Department of

Education—the same department where Eric's dad was an official—and the department that administered Pell Grants. According to Department of Education's website, "The Federal Pell Grant Program provides need-based grants to low-income undergraduate and certain post baccalaureate students to promote access to postsecondary education." At a time where America's youth needed to remain competitive in global education, and when the rising cost of debt was burdening middle-class families more than any other segment of the population, the Tea Party's education agenda made them as popular as ugly holiday sweaters.

In an *ABC News* column regarding Millennial student loan debt, Adam Levin said, "Congress needs to step up to the plate and start taking Millennials' concerns seriously, because their student debt burden, unlike Reagan's tax cuts, are going to trickle down throughout our economy, as the next generation finds itself unable to afford to buy houses, finance large purchases (like new cars) or even just make Black Friday actually black for retailers. If they can't find jobs, can't build good credit, can't achieve salary growth and continue to struggle under a massive debt burden from the second they start their adult lives, they aren't going to push the American economy to new heights, and we're all going to preside over its sputtering."

The article title warned, "Politicians: Ignore the Millennial Student Loan Crisis at Your Own Risk." In a plea for Washington to address solutions, it continued by saying, "It's time to look at solutions, like the ability of students to refinance their loans (as proposed by the Consumer Financial Protection Bureau) or even discharge them in bankruptcy. It's time to crack down on abuses, whether it's by non-bank student loan servicers operating with too little oversight or for-profit colleges that take students' money and provide little actual education or even not-for-profit colleges in which administrators too often seem to personally profit at the expense of students' education (and adjuncts' ability to earn a living wage). Because if politicians and regulators don't find some way to help our young people out, many of them may join them in the unemployment line sooner rather than later."

Millennial Voices on Education

In a survey I conducted with Millennials across the country, some of their most pressing issues were around having to pay off their high student loan debt and battling high unemployment/underemployment rates. Young people surveyed wondered if politicians were paying attention, and if any policies would address Millennial problems.

One evening, I received this very insightful testimonial from an old classmate of mine from my elementary school days who messaged me this:

> Hi Jamie! I think it's so great what you're doing, giving a voice to our generation. If you're interested, I'd like to tell you about my fiancé and me. By the time we marry in 2016, as we start a life as husband and wife, we will have a combined debt of half a million dollars. With which we both have received (will receive) a massive amount of education from: undergraduate, masters and doctorate degrees. Yet, he is unable to find work in the US and might have to travel abroad to Thailand to get a job! And as I will be graduating from medical school, I can imagine it will be challenging for me as well to get a position in the U.S. We are told, to follow our dreams no matter the cost. But $500,000 (which keeps growing due to our wonderful friend, 'interest') is extremely daunting and we will spend our lives paying off this debt. It makes me physically sick to think about it.

And it wasn't just those who were going to school that were struggling; it was also Millennials who graduated with expensive degrees who were now not only dealing with high student loan debt, but with an inability to find work to pay that student loan debt down. On top of that, they couldn't start their adult lives. Here is one example I was sent:

> I think much of my story just deals with a future that hasn't even happened yet.
>
> On paper, it looks as though I am on the trajectory toward a life of [financial] success: graduated from a state school with a B.S. in molecular, cell, and developmental biology, honors in the major; graduated from a private school with a master in public health, and even obtained a grant that paid for a substantial portion of my education (although not all); currently in a Ph.D. program at a graduate university. And my boyfriend appears to be on the same path to financial success: graduated with a history degree from a state school, went to law school, and passed the bar the first time. We've been called by some people as a 'power couple.'
>
> Although both of our families could be classified as 'comfortable' households, my boyfriend and I are not in any shape or form, comfortable financially. I do agree that we could be in a worse situation, but I don't think he and I ever considered that we would be where we are at the age of 27 and 26, respectively.
>
> After undergrad, my masters programs, and my Ph.D. program . . . I am drowning in close to $100,000 in loans . . . and that amount, I am sure, will continue to grow with about three or four more years left in my Ph.D. program. I accumulated debt during undergrad as an out of state student. I accumulated debt during my masters program because the grant didn't cover tuition costs for some of the semesters (can you believe that I accumulated close to $45,000 in debt just for attending 4 semesters at my private university?!). All of this because I

wanted to go to schools that I knew I could thrive in. Could I have chosen other schools that were cheaper and less costly? Absolutely, yes but I chose my happiness and well being over being debt-free. I refused to allow something like money rules my life. I am trying my best to stay positive and believe that my choices were the best for my life, my sanity, and even my soul . . . but I am not sure how I will feel once I get out of school and need to pay back these loans.

My boyfriend is in a better boat than I am, but still struggling. His family is a bit more 'comfortable' than my family as evidenced by the fact that he got out of all his schooling being debt-free. But, he is still trying to find a job after finding out he passed the bar last November. In an attempt to gain more experience (because every, single job wants at least 2 or 3 years of experience), he and I both agreed that he would work for free as a volunteer D.A. for one of the counties in Southern California. At what cost? That would mean that we live off my student loans (taking more out than I normally would) and living with his parents, who have been so kind to not charge us any rent, and there has always been food in the fridge and pantry.

I constantly keep telling myself:

'This is the best thing we can do right now.'

'This will pay off in the long run.'

'It's better to struggle now than later.'

'We could be in a worse situation.'

But. . . . you can imagine my worry about our financial situation: How long will my boyfriend be out of a job? We can't even get married or start the life we want because he doesn't have a job, and I am in debt. Will there be job openings for me? Will I able to afford starting a family? Will I be able to even afford a house, or will I have to live with my boyfriend's parents for the rest of my life? Oh my gosh, my kids! I can't even imagine the debt they will incur for college tuition and higher education. I'll probably still be paying off my own loans! We will never get to travel the world because of these loans, or the ongoing expenses we have to take-on because of being an "adult." The list of worries goes on and on and on.

It is humiliating in some regard. Knowing how accomplished you are compared to most of your peers, and yet you are struggling behind the scenes. Sometimes I feel like I should have chosen another career; one that just gets me in the field right away and gets money rolling in my account. So what if I can add a few abbreviations at the end of my name? Those abbreviations are costing me an arm and leg . . . but everyone, including my parents, told me that education will allow me much more freedom. But I have this unshakeable feeling that there is a ball and chain stuck to my leg that gets heavier and heavier each year. These are some of the negative thoughts I have.

At this point, I do want you to know how extremely humbled I am by this journey. Since graduating from college, I have experienced so much personal growth in mind, body, and spirit, and the struggles I have endured (not just financial) have definitely lead me to a life of humility and spirituality. I do realize, as I mentioned, how our situation is better than most people. We have a roof over our heads, food always at hand; parents who we can fall back on; have the opportunity to attend schools most people dream of. I always struggle with the aforementioned negative thoughts that plague my mind, but I will always keep hope that this was the path I was meant to take. Why should I allow money to get in the way of my dreams?

I am just hoping that it WILL pay off in the end. And I am hoping that I will be able to keep these same positive thoughts once those notices of payment start coming in. I also continue to pray for everyone in the world struggling, because I know that there are young people, like my boyfriend and me, who are struggling more than we are. And if I feel like I'm drowning, I am sure they feel like they are close to death. I also shudder to think about those young people who are too scared to go after their dreams of getting an education because of money. Who are those amazing young people and how could they have helped our world?

I received another testimonial by a young man who claimed that he not only had student loan debt, but he also had a degree that didn't prepare him for the workforce. He talked about how public school curriculum is so outdated and how bubbling answers on standardized tests did not prepare him for the real world:

In an evolving world, you need an evolving curriculum. The style in which we are taught should engage students and get us active. You are asked to be passive, and then all of a sudden you are asked to get active in the workforce and to produce eight hours a day. It took a long time to learn to sit down for eight hours a day, and now I need to be active eight hours a day. I used to passively take in information and have been trained to do that, however now I need to retrain myself to be active. Boys want to run around and do things and engage. We are told we have ADHD because we can't sit down for eight hours a day—which is unnatural. If we're lucky enough to master it, then we master something that has no use in the workforce. If you're a sales person you need to produce new leads and new sales. If you're an analyst, you have to produce summaries and documents explaining your analysis, you constantly have to produce. And that is not what they ask us to do in school. They ask us to understand, understand, understand. You sit 16 years of your life 'understanding' and passively watching things, and then you are supposed to flip a switch and start producing massive amounts of content. You didn't make anything in school, you didn't work in a manufacturing plant. Except maybe a mid-term or final paper that's due, which you struggle to do in one night, but that is just about the only production you have to do prior to joining the workforce.

The numerous tests we had to take are even passive because you are just taking in information, and you just have to bubble in an answer. Because my father was a professor, I basically was a student—constantly—24 hours a day. Your mind is expanded beyond everyone else because you have someone at home constantly lecturing. They speak for extended periods of time, and kids become good listeners and understanding. I then decided, I was going to become the best passive observer I can be. I am now able to take massive amounts of information about things. I'm like an encyclopedia because I can retain and add to my base of knowledge of things that I've already learned. I can analyze and interpret, regurgitate and repeat.

But when it came to having to produce things in the real world once I got into the workforce, it was like, where did that come from? I've never had to do that. That's totally new. It feels like a little bit of a struggle, and the problem is, we don't like to do things we're not good at. Anything you're new to, you're usually not good at. Repetition is the mother of skill, and unfortunately, our school system was just asking us to repeat tests—not truly create, act or produce anything. I don't think people realize this was a huge transition for our generation We basically went from passive observer to active producer, and simultaneously, we are going from a high standard of living to the real world of what you can actually afford, which for our generation's case, is a drastically lower standard of living.

Despite receiving various views, one core issue remained a consistent problem: education in America. Problems with education were wide ranging and included: lack of sufficient education, the price of education, and even too much formal education for the practical needs of certain job opportunities that punished "over-qualified" candidates. Another common complaint mentioned was the reality that the education of many Millennials didn't prepare them for the realities of the workplace they were serving. The point is that whatever the specifics of a Millennial's problem, responses when asked what their major life issues were, most in some way pointed to education.

View from the Top: President Eduardo Ochoa Speaks on U.S. Education

Meanwhile, in my personal life, I was able to get front row seats to this pressing issue so many Millennials were concerned about.

I couldn't think of a better person to ask for an interview than Eric's father, who was the former chief advisor on higher education to President Obama—Assistant Secretary Eduardo Ochoa. I thought he would be a wonderful resource in answering some of the survey questions I had asked young people.

By the time we sat down for our interview (which happened in 2013), Dr. Ochoa had finished two years with the Obama Administration. He was now appointed by the California State University Board of Trustees as President of California State University Monterey Bay (CSUMB)—a small state university on the central coast of California.

Our interview took place over Skype. President Ochoa was in his home, and I was in Hawai'i for reasons that will be detailed later in Chapter Seven. CSUMB is an interesting campus that Ochoa was chosen to lead. CSUMB sits on what used to be the Army facilities of Fort Ord, sandwiched between the very wealthy communities of Carmel and the largely migrant farming community of Salinas, on the other side of the "Lettuce Curtain." Ochoa's Argentinean-American background made him an ideal leader for the campus. Seeing that just over half of CSUMB students are first generation to attend college, with Latinos comprising about a third of the total student body, Ochoa's Latino roots and well-educated background made him a role model to the fastest growing segment of the U.S. population. When I say Dr. Ochoa is well educated, I don't say that lightly. With a total of three degrees—from Reed College, Columbia University, and the New School for Social Research, respectively—Dr. Ochoa's undergraduate degree is in physics, with a second major in philosophy, and the advanced degrees are in nuclear engineering and economics. A veteran of the Cal State system for some 30 years, his wide range of experience from California to D.C. made him the perfect candidate to answer all my questions.

The region he serves is also known as "Steinbeck Country." Monterey County was home to the Pulitzer Prize-winning author John Steinbeck, who prided himself in writing about the experiences of struggle during the Great Depression. While in the same geographic location, Dr. Ochoa and I discussed a parallel topic—the greatest economic collapse since the Great Depression. Over 70 years later, President Ochoa was now serving the same community Steinbeck had written about. It is rumored that while Steinbeck was working on his manuscript for his award-winning novel, *Grapes of Wrath*, he famously said, "I want to put a tag of shame on the greedy bastards who are responsible for this [The Great Depression and its effects]."

As a writer who admires Steinbeck's work, I wasn't feeling so different, either. But I vowed to stay objective in the interview.

As our interview began, I cited that in the latest international student evaluations published by the Program for International Student Assessment among 34 countries, the United States "performed below average in mathematics . . . and is ranked 26 in math, 17 in reading, and 21 in science." Some of the other findings include: "The U.S. spends more per student than most countries, but this has not translated into better performance. Students in the United States have particular weaknesses in performing mathematics tasks with higher cognitive demands, such as taking real-world situations, translating them into mathematical equations, and interpreting mathematical aspects into real-world problems." Lastly, it found that "socio-economic background has a significant impact on student performance, . . . with some 15% variation in student performance explained by this . . . Disadvantaged students show less engagement, drive, motivation and self-beliefs."

In light of these statistics, I asked Dr. Ochoa his overall view on education in America:

Eduardo Ochoa: Some of the recent and most commonly stated statistics are that the rest of the world is gaining on us. When you look at international tests in the K-12 space, we are not the top performing country. We're not the head of the pack. The education level of college aged students now ages 25–34 who are recent graduates are performing lower than previous generations. We are losing ground.

However, there are caveats to that fact. For example, when it comes to the education levels of young people being lower than previous generations, this finding tends to ignore the fact that, unlike other countries, in the United States people continue to educate themselves in their later years; whereas, in other countries, they go to school and then go directly into the workforce. That's it. They don't continue to go to school. So, if you actually compared younger people in the U.S. now with the education of older people back when they were young themselves, you will find that you don't have that disparity. When it comes to educational levels of those on K-12 tests, that is also a limited picture on the state of education. It is part of the picture, but it is not the whole picture.

For example, many of the countries that do very well in those, like Singapore and Korea, continue to look to the U.S. as a model. And in fact, they recognize they have to go beyond focusing on STEM and technical education, and bring in more of the liberal arts like the United States has. They recognize that the growth they experience up to now has been based on imitation and adopting innovations that were developed elsewhere. If they want to lead in the global economy, they have to have those kinds of elements in their education system that foster innovation and creativity.

Innovation and creativity happen to be the most powerful elements of education in America. With all the problems we have when it comes to our K-12 system, high school system, and preparing students for college, our students who do graduate actually experience an educational system that fosters more independent thinking and innovation than our competitors do.

Things are not as bad as it sounds, but human beings continue to improve, and in that regard, we have hit a flat. President Obama's goal of making it practically universal that everyone has some form of post-secondary education or training after high school is very much the right direction.

It has been a concern that states have been disinvesting in funding higher education for a number of years, and the share of tuition that students are paying has grown. The lack of funding is problematic because when you look at the earnings differential between college-educated workers and those who only have high school education or less, and their differential rates on employment, it has never been more important to have post-secondary education than today. That tells you what we are doing to promote higher education is very necessary. That is the direction we have to go in order to maintain our competitive edge.

Jamie Borromeo: Do you have a more optimistic view of education in America?

EO: I think I'm neither Pollyannaish about it nor am I a Cassandra. I don't think the sky is falling but I think we have issues we have to deal with. First of all, overall, we still have the best higher education system in the world. The problem with it is, some of our schools are better than any, and then there are other segments of our education system that are not really where they should be. We have bigger disparities than we should have, and the quality of education and the success of the students have in some ways mirrored where we are in America right now across the board. There are growing disparities in segments of American society—growing inequality in America.

JB: What segments are you talking about?

EO: I think that the public K-12 system, by and large, is having problems. I think we are not demanding enough from the system when they graduate from high school. Too many students are not ready to do college-level work. Nowadays, really, being college ready is the same thing as being career ready. The skills you need to get through college are the same skills you need to be successful in almost any occupation: a greater emphasis on the use of technology, understanding of numbers, math, and communication skills. All the things that prepare you for college prepare you for the workforce, as well.

JB: I saw the Tea Party was against Common Core Standards.

EO: Right now, the Tea Party phenomenon and the right wing of the Republican Party seems to be having such a disproportionate effect on the party. They are pretty much against anything that Obama is for. They are even against policies that Republicans had supported before.

Healthcare . . . Cap and Trade . . . The idea of common core standards was developed by the Association of Governors. There has been consensus since the days of No Child Left Behind. What we are getting now is an anti-Obama obsession.

To give it a little more substance, the Common Core Standards recognized if we are going to be globally competitive, we have to have a baseline level of competency among our graduates. They were developed on a consensus basis, endorsed by the National Governors Association and the organization that brings together all the state school officers from across the country. They are very broad standards that include math primarily and English, as well. It still is up to each local school board and state to implement standards within a specific curriculum. There is a long tradition in the U.S. of local school board control of education, which frankly, has become problematic. That creates wide disparities in the quality standards of education that students get at K-12 level. You will have very affluent districts that will spend a lot of money on their programs. It's basically well-educated parents that understand science and math, and they don't get hung up on Creationism and those sorts of things. Then there are other school districts that are extremely conservative and/or underprivileged that are more interested in placating their ideologies than preparing students for a 21st century economy.

JB: Where are we today with the Common Core Standards from the federal level?

EO: The federal government does not require Common Core Standards. There are some programs that the Department of Education funds for K-12, where we make sure they are high quality standards, but they don't mandate what requirements they have to be. Clearly, the Common Core Standards would fit the bill. But they are not requiring that it be those specific standards.

JB: So are you saying the Department of Education suggests certain standards for local school boards?

EO: No, they don't even do that. There is not a list of acceptable standards. They just have descriptive language that says they have to have high quality standards. And they list some general attributes and features of what they should accomplish but not what they should be.

JB: What was your role like as Assistant Secretary of Education?

EO: Well, we were talking about K-12, but my role was in higher education, of course, but it was similar there. In K-12, there is local community control. At the higher education and postsecondary levels, you typically have state control for four-year institutions, and in California, you have local control for community colleges. But in either case, the federal government is out of the picture. So the federal government's role is to provide funds to support education and promote access and equity. Those are typically the roles.

JB: When you say access and equity, what do you mean by that?

EO: It means that we had programs like the Trio Programs that help disadvantaged students do well in school. We have programs that are capacity building for institutions tailored to minority-serving institutions, we had a program called Fulbright Hayes that gave scholarships to faculty to develop greater competencies, and we had programs that supported international and foreign language education, which was motivated, in part, by the Cold War and the need for the U.S. to understand the rest of the world. And then, we have the big elephant in the room, which is the federal student aid program. The two biggest [programs] being the Pell grants and the direct student loans. And that represents a huge investment on the part of the federal government, and the only requirement that is tied to those loans is that the schools that the students attend should be accredited. They should be accredited by an agency that is recognized by the Department of Education. So one of our jobs was to accredit the accreditors, in fact.

JB: You talked about federal student aid programs that are very relevant to the Millennial Generation. Can you talk a little bit about work you did around that?

EO: Our main effort was preserving Pell Grants. In spite of the fact that we were in a recession, as an economist, I believe, like most of my colleagues, we actually need to increase spending to compensate for the drop in private sector demand. Washington became obsessed with deficits, which obviously get worse in a recession, because they are supposed to get worse in a recession. The government is supposed to be counter-cyclical. They tried to look for ways to reduce the deficit, or at least not make it worse, so that created pressure on the Pell Grant program, and so we were trying to preserve it. We were trying to do some triage on it. We ended up getting rid of summer Pell Grants because they were not quite as effective as the ones during the academic year in terms of bang for the buck, but mostly worked at holding the line at the maximum Pell Grant award. Pell Grants are absolutely great. They work; they do the job they are intended to do. And the argument for subsidizing any kind of education, higher education in particular, is that the returns to society for more educated citizens make it a worthwhile investment. If you look at the California State University (CSU) system's analysis, the state, in terms of dollars spent on subsidizing higher education, it showed for every dollar that the state spent on the CSU, it received over $4 back in increased tax revenues, let alone, gross state product. Just in terms of state revenue, it actually more than paid for itself.

JB: Are you saying there is opposition to Pell Grants, and if so, what were they saying?

EO: Well, we started to hear a lot of stories, like what you're writing about in your book, about Millennials having trouble in this economy. People have jumped to the conclusion that since students are having a hard time—which is true for what it is worth—that this means college isn't worth it and it's a waste of money. Which of course, is not the case, because if you don't have a college education, you will do far far worse in this economy than if you do have an education.

JB: What did the opposition say?

EO: They were saying that it wasn't worth it because people were unemployed when they came out of college, so we wasted their money when they graduated and a lot of them didn't graduate, so we were throwing money down a rat hole. Even though people made that argument, the biggest argument was that we just couldn't afford it. It was the deficit reduction that concerned them most.

JB: An issue frequently raised by young people is the tremendous student loan debt facing them after receiving a degree. One Millennial wrote to me and said, "By the time my fiancé and I marry in 2015, we will have a combined student loan debt of half a million dollars. We both are in med school, but don't believe we will be able to afford to practice in the U.S. We are looking to move to Thailand after we graduate."

A graduate school student wrote in and said, "My boyfriend and I cannot afford to buy a house or even get married because all of our family savings has gone to education, and neither of us can find jobs despite having degrees. We have put our personal lives on hold because of this economy."

How do you feel about the two scenarios?

EO: Let me talk specifically about these two examples you gave. First, the two in med school: Doctors in the U.S. make a lot more than doctors in other countries. Ever since I've been in this country, for decades, they have been artificially limiting the number of people who can become doctors by limiting the number of slots for med school—to the point where people end up going abroad to med school because it's hard to get into programs here. If you do that—if you create artificial scarcity—that makes the few available slots in medical school very valuable, and people are willing to pay tons of money [for them]. They are charging you huge amounts of money because they can, because they artificially limit the numbers. That's like a cabbie trying to get a medallion in New York. It's not inherently that valuable, but there aren't that many, so that's the reason why med school is very expensive. So, if you both are going to med school, I'm not surprised that you're piling up a huge debt. So, now one of the things they are caught in—the question is: will doctors continue making the kind of money they did in the past? And healthcare costs are rising so much that there are pressures developing in that sector, and in that sector that may bend the cost curve. And so, to the extent that the new healthcare system succeeds in limiting the rise of healthcare costs, at some point or another, it's going to affect how much doctors make. Doctors are going to make less. And the dilemma is, if you are caught in a situation where you paid the premium to get in that market, because of the high value of getting a degree in the past, but then by the time you get there you're not making that money, you get caught in a bind. Eventually, when doctors' incomes fall to a more reasonable level, comparable to other professions, then medical schools are not going to be able to charge as much because it won't be as attractive of a proposition then. If you're caught in the wrong place at the wrong time, then you could be caught in a squeeze.

Now the other one: I think that you have to look at what they majored in and what kind of jobs are they looking for. You have several things going there: you have the cyclical economy—yes—when you're caught in the wrong part of a cycle, you can have problems of getting that first job—and that's critical. Secondly, if you major in something that does not have a strong demand, in a straight forward field that flows out of that major, you have to get more creative on how to apply your abilities into a different field. And that's where getting a career consultant—someone to help you think out of the box of what's possible, writing resumes that emphasize your skills and abilities, and not your specific content so much, but what sorts of things you could do—that would be helpful. There's no question that coming out of the wrong part of the economic cycle can hurt you. And it's cold comfort to know that it's cyclical.

While our Skype interview was coming to an end, Eric was there with his father during the interview, and he chimed in on a solution that I found to be rather useful. He said:

People that come out of college typically have an idea of being in something glamorous, and there are very few jobs available in those fields. But there are positions available that pay very well for types of jobs that people don't normally associate with college degrees. For example, I was reading about the company Caterpillar. You can make up to six figures operating machinery for them, which is a job you wouldn't think to apply for as a college graduate, but can pay you more and offer more security than what most people end up getting as their first job. If young people open their mind to careers they never thought of, it could pay more than an office job. If they were aware of it, you would have more demand for that position.

And there it was, the balanced insight I needed to feel the hope. I'm glad Dr. Ochoa provided insight that was not doom and gloom, yet not glowing. Yes, we did have curriculum and structural issues with Department of Education. And yes, students had a ton of student loan debt. But having a degree versus not having a degree still had its benefits. And, there were still some career opportunities—just maybe not in industries we would have expected. And, despite our low testing scores, overall, America still had a competitive edge in education when it came to innovation and creativity—characteristics of American education that other countries envied.

Lastly, the most comforting part from President Ochoa's interview was that this long recovery was cyclical, which meant it would eventually end. What goes up must come down, and what is down—the U.S. economy and the feeling we get when we think of all that student loan debt—will eventually lift.

It was time for me to find out if Millennials who did have higher education degrees could apply that very expensive knowledge they bought through tuition to some solutions.

This is when I moved on in my travels to New York to help the Clinton Foundation with their Millennium Network Event. I co-chaired their New York City donor event that would engage the next generation of leaders in the philanthropic work of the Clinton Foundation. There, I would find answers to a recent phenomenon that could possibly provide jobs for our generation: social entrepreneurship.

CHAPTER 5

New York, 2011:
Hope from a New Generation
of Business Leaders

"The critical ingredient is getting off your butt and doing something. It's as simple as that. A lot of people have ideas, but there are few who decide to do something about them now. Not tomorrow. Not next week. But today. The true entrepreneur is a doer, not a dreamer."

—Nolan Bushnell

R ockefeller Center had silver and gold flags waving in the winter wind. A chilly 20-something degrees, I looked up at the beautiful Christmas tree and was dazzled by the holiday spirit that filled Manhattan.

It was December 2011, and Eric and I were visiting New York to co-chair the Clinton Foundation Millennium Network event at Terminal 5 on West 56th Street.

The purpose of the evening was to engage the next generation of leaders and philanthropists in the work of the Clinton Foundation. Some of our California friends who were transplants to Manhattan joined us for the donor reception that night. We were greeted with an open bar, a buffet of sushi, a guest appearance by comedian Paul Rudd, and entertainment by the band, The Fray. President Clinton impressed my young friends and me with his party-throwing skills; it certainly rivaled some of the best college parties we ever attended (despite a beer-pong table not being included).

A big screen was above the stage, featuring a slide show of the all the work of the Foundation, with quotes by President Clinton rotating through the slide show. As I was standing in the cocktail line, I read a very important quote by the President that said, "I really believe this generation of young people has more power than any before it to make a real difference in our world. Together we can build a future with more partners, fewer enemies, and shared prosperity."

As the crowd quieted and the music stopped, Chelsea Clinton came up to the stage to introduce her father, saying he was "the biggest source of her inspiration." He certainly was mine, as well.

President Clinton stepped on the stage and wooed the crowd in a "Clintonesque" way that only he could do. As he thanked Paul Rudd, Chelsea, and his new son-in-law, Mark Mezvinsky, he charmingly excused himself for his lengthy remarks by saying, "I know I'm the only thing standing between you and The Fray. I'll try to keep it short."

President Clinton went on to talk about the mission of his foundation, and why he found it important that Millennials were getting involved.

The Clinton Foundation's mission is to build partnerships with NGOs, businesses, governments, and individuals around key areas, which include: improving global health, increasing opportunity for women and girls, reducing childhood obesity and preventable diseases, creating economic opportunity and growth, and addressing the effects of climate change.

President Clinton housed a special initiative—just for young people—under his Millennium Network to engage future leaders and philanthropists in his work.

With his Southern drawl and ability to reach audience members on a real level, the President spoke to the crowd of young people like an uncle imparting knowledge. "When you get older, you don't feel old until you look in the mirror. But you won't really feel old if you have something to look forward to. And this, I do look forward to because it's fun, it's a privilege, and well, it's challenging. Most importantly, I want to figure out how to solve some of these global problems. Non-government groups have big advantages over private sector and government. We don't have any quarterly pressure to perform, like the private sector."

What President Clinton was talking about was the fact that in today's capitalism, the pressure to make profits is the sole purpose of most corporations. His new role in the Clinton Foundation was simply to find solutions and fund-raise, and just enough to get the job done. His focus didn't have to be appeasing voters nor shareholders, things that elected officials and corporations needed to worry about.

But what if profit doesn't have to be the only priority of private enterprise? With so many non-profit groups and foundations strapped for cash in this long recovery, business could play a role in solving our societal issues, too. What if businesses could turn a profit *and* give back to the world through their companies?

If there is any time in history where the societal contribution of a corporation could become equally as important as turning a profit, this might be that time. With Millennials more eager to start their own businesses, this could be the generation that requires a business with meaning *and* contribution.

President Clinton: Back to Work

President Clinton's book *Back to Work: Why We Need Smart Government for a Strong Economy* was published the same year I co-chaired his foundation's event. Reading it, I was engrossed in his savvy solutions for alleviating America's high unemployment rates and what government could do to fix it.

In his epilogue, Clinton acknowledged that one of the main reasons America should get back to work is so that we can get "back in the future business" for America's youth.

"In a Gallup poll in spring of 2011, fewer than half of Americans surveyed believed the current generation of young adults will have a better life than their parents . . . young people are altering their career plans, putting off marriage, and downsizing their dreams," said the President. "I can understand the pessimism of the young," he continued. "After all, we've been mired in this current mess for a significant portion of their lives. But giving up is not a strategy for success. Downsizing budgets may be necessary, but downsizing dreams is a decision to be disappointed."

With 46 clear prescriptions for what it would take for the U.S. to get money flowing, the President pointed to small business as one of the ways to speed up the recovery.

Small Business: America's *Real* Job Creators

The first part of the President's recommendations focused on policies regarding the financial crisis, taxes, subsidies, production, exports and international competition. The second half had clear recommendations for job creation and entrepreneurship.

In number 33, "Increase the role of the Small Business Administration (SBA)," President Clinton cites that "Nearly thirty million small businesses have created most of America's new jobs over the last fifteen years, generated more than half our nonfarm GDP, and paid the salaries of more than half our private sector workers."

While the common rhetoric from Republicans during recent elections was that corporations were "job creators," it seems the numbers President Clinton provided show that it is actually *small businesses in America* that are the real job creators.

In an article by *Entrepreneur Magazine* called, "Why Americans Love Small Business," it said, "A July 2012, Rasmussen survey found that 57 percent of American voters think small business owners create more jobs and generate more economic growth than either big businesses or the government."

Despite this, the President accurately points out that, "Pepperdine University reported that more than half the small businesses surveyed said that their attempts to get more capital has been unsuccessful and that banks had denied 60% of small-business loan applications this year."

While corporations have been too big to fail, America's small businesses have become too small to lend to. The widening gap between corporate America and main street small businesses has hurt small business' ability to hire new employees—further lagging our long recovery.

"According to Gallup's chief economist," President Clinton says, "40 percent of small businesses are hiring fewer people than they need. That's when the SBA is supposed to step in, offering loan guarantees of 50 to 85 percent for bank loans to small businesses, with 100 percent guarantees for disaster loans. Even when SBA does offer guarantees, small businesses often find loans hard to come by."

Clinton, at the end of his paragraph, has no problem sticking it to financial institutions. "Despite benefiting from government bailouts and sitting on huge amounts of money, most banks have proved remarkably reluctant to make even guaranteed loans to small businesses."

I had seen President Clinton effectively move the agenda for small businesses under his leadership when he was in office. When I was growing up, I remember my mother and father being integral to the minority business agenda of the President in the 1990's. Part of multiple minority business owner delegations invited to the White House, my parents provided recommendations to Clinton's Small Business Administration and to his Minority Business Development Agency (MBDA). Under Clinton's presidency, he furthered America's small business agenda by elevating SBA to a cabinet position. This contributed to doubling the amount of SBA loans processed and increasing minority and women business loans three times over.

Crowd funding came next on President Clinton's agenda. "Crowd-funding is the term used for receiving small sums of money over the Internet. It allows start-ups and small businesses that are seeking to expand to raise money directly from individuals without going through a financial middleman. This has real potential to fill the financial gap many small entrepreneurs face if they can't get conventional venture capital or a bank loan."

He went on to explain that a rather outdated law from the 1930s prohibits small businesses from being able to crowd-fund because an expensive regulatory process, which only very wealthy and knowledgeable investors can currently benefit from, would cost an entrepreneur far too much. So while crowd funding has a regulatory setback as a stumbling block, it remains a crucial tool for small business owners.

Micro-lending, another form of financing that President Clinton is a huge fan of, became a reality for the underserved, and when Mohammed Unis started Grameen Bank in 1983, the micro-lending program that gave poor people a chance at entrepreneurship, the idea of the "social entrepreneur" began to catch fire. Unis had transformed the prospects of upward mobility not only for his country of India, but for poor people all over the world. Grameen Bank was awarded a Nobel Peace Prize in 2006, and it inspired some people within the Millennial Generation to make changing lives the new bottom line in their business.

Generations ME ME MEaning

Barry Salzberg, the Global Chief Executive Officer of Deloitte Touche Tohmatsu Limited, wrote an article in 2012 called, "What Millennials Want Most: A Career That Actually Matters." He says, "Never mind the still sluggish job market. In their insistence on social principle, many Millennials are not driven by money or success in quite the way their parents were. This generation wants to know what your organization stands for in improving society, what it stands for in action, as opposed to blowing smoke. Millennials want to know how they will make a positive difference in the world if they join your business, not by wearing a colorful T-shirt on a special project once a year, but in their actual work."

He delights in asking readers the following, "Did I mention that this media-savvy generation is also jaded and suspicious? Unimpressed by title, well traveled, and immune to P.R. in the old sense? To anyone who imagines their heartstrings can be nimbly plucked, good luck."

Salzberg continues his piece by acknowledging that high unemployment and lack of training has been a global Millennial problem by saying, "Yes, employment remains a challenge, in the U.S. and especially in parts of Europe suffering from double-digit unemployment, such as Spain, Portugal, Italy, and Greece. True, more needs to be done to align education and training with today's jobs, and my organization, among many, is striving to do just that. But to be realistic, it will take the bulldozer of business, going at full throttle, to get us out of the ditch."

He closes with an accurate solution by advising his *Fortune 500* counterparts, "To do that effectively, business needs to move past the denial stage and get everyone on board, including the new generation of workers, with all their energy, curiosity, new skills, and passion."

We Want to Be a Part of Something Bigger

In a piece titled, "Social Entrepreneurship: How Millennials Can be the Next Greatest Generation," blogger David Murray shared with readers his experience attending the Columbia Social Enterprise Conference hosted by Columbia University's business school in October 2013.

The forum featured a company, MPOWERD, which is a social enterprise that manufactures Luci, "a small, lightweight inflatable device that captures solar energy during the day, and emits it at night."

The problem MPOWERD was facing, despite their innovative solution for the "1.3 billion people who lack electricity at night," was that they were not turning a large enough profit. They were not a non-government organization or charity, so the CEO asked the audience at the conference to help solve his dilemma of wanting to provide this social good, but still make money doing it.

Among the college students attending, the guest audience gave the CEO free consulting. In the breakout groups, everyone pitched in with ideas. From "partnering with international charities or outdoor retailers, to creating 'sister schools' where American students would buy a Luci and learn about solar energy, and in turn fundraise to share the product with a school in the developing world," these young people freely offered many valuable ideas—and he didn't even have to hire McKinsey. Young people are willing to offer their talent if they know it makes a difference. Companies that get that will certainly thrive once Millennials become leaders.

Generation Sell

In an Op-Ed featured in *The New York Times* in November 2011, author William Deresiewicz speaks of his observation of this new generation of budding entrepreneurs: "Here's what I see around me, in the city and the culture: food carts, 20-somethings selling wallets made from recycled plastic bags, boutique pickle companies, techie start-ups, Kickstarter, urban-farming supply stores and bottled water that wants to save the planet. Today's ideal social form is not the commune or the movement or even the individual creator as such; it's the small business. Every artistic or moral aspiration—music, food, good works, what have you—is expressed in those terms."

He then observes the social entrepreneurship of this generation saying, "Bands are still bands, but now they're little businesses, as well: self-produced, self-published, self-managed . . . Non-profits are still hip, but students don't dream about joining one, they dream about starting one. In any case, what's really hip is social entrepreneurship—companies that try to make money responsibly, then give it all away."

A good example of this trend in business and new wave of young, social entrepreneurs is a business called Purpose. "Purpose creates 21st century movements," the website says. "We deploy the collective power of millions of people to help solve major global problems. To do this, we develop and launch our own technology-driven social movements from concept to execution, using our model of movement entrepreneurship, and we partner with existing organizations to help them apply movement theory and practice to their own work."

From civil liberties and LGBT rights to aged care, gun safety, and global income inequality, Purpose provides strategies for its clients that "combine emerging technology with key insights from political organizing, behavioral economics, storytelling, organizational strategy, and visual and interaction design." With clients such as Google, Ben &

Jerry's and the ACLU, Purpose assists high net-worth clients with big social movements.

So who exactly is the social innovation rock star that started all this? The CEO of Purpose is Jeremy Heimans, a native of Australia, whose entrepreneurial skills and love for social justice started at a very young age.

In an interview with *Forbes Magazine*, Heimans says, "From the age of 8, I was running media campaigns on global issues back home in Australia. I was ever so slightly precocious. I would meet with senior Australian government officials, including the prime minister and foreign minister, proposing various solutions to third world debt and malnutrition."

He jokingly added, "I tried very hard to make peace and environmental studies compulsory in all schools. My parents didn't know quite what to do with me."

Embodying all the elements of a Millennial social entrepreneur, Heimans emphasizes the importance of "creating both economic and social value at the same time." He says, "It is critically important that every sector in society orients itself to solving the world's big challenges . . . Perhaps the most encouraging trend is that through technology people are realizing how much agency they actually have. Technology has revolutionized the way we eat, live, communicate, socialize, learn and do. We see enormous potential to create lasting positive change in the way the world works by doing what we are doing."

Jobs with a Purpose?

What if entrepreneurship were taught widely and a movement of social enterprise could effectively put Millennials back to work and allow us to work on things that we feel deeply and passionately about? Because Millennials seek meaning in our lives more than material wealth, could this cultural shift reshape capitalism in America? Can Millennials do what we love outside of a cubicle, and make money doing it?

In 2012, Heimans co-authored an article in the *Huffington Post* titled, "Join the Insurgency Against the Job Crisis." In it, he states, "We need to redefine what 'good jobs' mean and then create them. We need to look at the margins and start from the bottom up. This requires a shift in our attitudes and policies in support of the economic insurgents, agile, disruptive start-up enterprises, instead of continuing to prop up the same incumbent institutions of subsidized big businesses and crony capitalists."

He emphatically says, "Good jobs come from supporting more companies that embody new economy models and deliver social and economic value at the same time."

Heimans, in his closing paragraphs of the article about the job crisis, says, "Without reforming the way we finance our politics, we have little hope in making the policy changes we need to address the jobs crisis because the old incumbents will always have more influence than the bottom-up insurgents. That is why we have recently formed unPAC. org in partnership with United Republic and Lessig to advocate for new rules to counter the corrupting influence of money in politics."

He closed with an Albert Einstein quote, "'We can't solve problems by using the same kind of thinking we used when we created them.' We need new thinking and new politics to build the networked commons and solve the jobs crisis."

I couldn't have agreed with Heimans more that a new way of thinking was needed when it came to politics—and in my own life.

By the end of 2011, I had a new problem: I was, yet again, in a successful position, but not taking care of my personal life. A certified workaholic by that time, D.C. culture put my ambition in overdrive. I was now sitting on the advisory council of the U.S. Department of Energy's small business group. I was invited by Congress to provide testimonials on America's small businesses. I was featured in magazines, invited on radio shows, and I was invited by the Democratic National Committee to speak on behalf of America's small businesses during President Obama's presidential run for a second term. I was a guest speaker traveling from Boston to Manhattan, Manhattan to Philadelphia. I was giving speeches all over the East Coast, promoting workforce development and entrepreneurship for young people. Our company was thriving, but my personal life took a nosedive. I was emotionally drained. My Blackberry would send me messages at odd hours, with the Type A, East Coast visitor wanting to pay a visit to our downtown luxury apartment on the corner of Third and Massachusetts in Washington, D.C. Visitors no longer came to pay a visit as a friend—they wanted my contacts.

Eric and I soon realized we could obtain worldly success in that environment, but we would have to continue to sacrifice our personal lives. The type of life we had to live and the types of people we had to be would not have been worth it.

And besides, I missed my family. I missed my friends. I missed my nieces and nephews. I missed my grandmother, *Lola*.

I was ready to return to the sunny state of California.

CHAPTER 6

Los Angeles, 2012: From Main Street to Wall Street

"Minorities are well on their way to becoming the majority of our workforce and our entrepreneurial economy. It's well established that small business is the biggest source of job creation and wealth generation to the U.S. economy; Therefore, priority needs to be given to support entrepreneurship . . . The emphasis needs to be on development of minority businesses."

—Dr. Leonard Greenhalgh

T wo years after I had lived on the East Coast, I found myself back in my hometown of Diamond Bar, which is a small suburb in Los Angeles County. Home to famous people like rapper Snoop Dogg and Olympic soccer gold-medalist Alex Morgan, Diamond Bar was a charming affluent town that bordered three major counties in Southern California—Los Angeles, Orange and San Bernardino—I was in the middle of a city in a sprawling suburbia that felt like a fantasy land. It was a city where people didn't seem to worry about income. There were no homeless people peeing on the bus stop pole like they used to in front of my Capitol Hill apartment. There was no visible sign of poverty the way my D.C. neighborhood regularly had panhandlers on the corner.

One day, I went to visit my old journalism teacher, Mr. Roubian, from my former alma mater, Diamond Bar High School. As I was waiting in front of the campus to sign in with the front office for a guest pass, I saw a high school student pull up to the curb in his Range Rover. His key still in the ignition and engine still turned on, with his doors unlocked and windows wide open, he left the car running in front of the campus for minutes. Between the time that I entered the front office to the time the front desk receptionist finally signed me in, the entire five minutes, that Range Rover was still sitting there empty with no driver and the car still on.

One of two things would have happened to this young man and his car if he happened to live in a different neighborhood—perhaps even my neighborhood in D.C.: 1) He would have gotten jumped for being so flashy with all his name brands—or for simply having a Range Rover, or 2) Someone would have immediately stolen his car and possibly even shot him, depending on which part of Southeast he was in and how he conducted himself.

Despite being very surprised that I was the least bit culture-shocked to be back in the town that I grew up in, a part of me was happy to be home. I was so happy, in fact, that the last neighborhood that my family lived in as a nuclear unit, I decided to make my own again after ten years of being away. I lived down the street from my family's old property. Everything from my childhood shops, grocery stores, and hair salon to the gas station—and more importantly—my grandmother's house, were only minutes away. They were all accessible through one main street that runs right through the small city that was named, of course, Diamond Bar Boulevard. This was *my* Main Street. And I was about to find out that my childhood Main Street was dramatically affected by Wall Street.

When I started to look for old childhood friends, they had moved out of houses they grew up in, or their families were forced to sell in the recession. They had all moved inland to cities that used to be considered cow towns. One girlfriend told me, "I wish I could afford to live in the city we grew up in, but I can't afford to live in Diamond Bar. I'm kind of sad that my kids can't even afford to go to the schools that I did."

Many Millennials looking to start their adult lives had to move 15–20 miles outside of their hometown to be able to afford the cost of living. And if they didn't move, it was because they were living with their mom and dad.

Some of my friends had children already, and they were sharing the challenges of having both parents work because babysitting costs were so expensive. "It doesn't make sense for me to work," one girlfriend said in disappointment. "With the amount daycare costs for two children, we actually save more money by just having one of us work."

Minority Majority

Although there were new faces, new shops and new roads that were paved, one thing about my hometown did not change: My main street was still majority minority. Almost 60% of my high school was Asian, with Korean Americans the top racial demographic. I was used to a diverse classroom where there were no color lines. I started to read up on the changing demographics in the United States, and I found out that by 2043, the rest of America will look just like my main street: ethnic minorities will be the majority. The Black, Latino, Asian American, and Native American populations will exceed the number of Caucasians in America for the first time.

Studies have shown that communities of color have historically had lower graduation rates, lower lifetime incomes, lower homeownership rates, and are not traditionally in leadership positions in corporate boardrooms or have minority elected officials representing them. The City of Diamond Bar is an anomaly in the sense that it fares very well in student performance, median income, and home ownership despite being majority minority.

With the exception of cities like Diamond Bar, this trend got me thinking, and rather concerned: If historically underserved communities will become the majority in America, wouldn't that mean that the majority of Americans would then be underserved? Would that mean that the majority of Americans would not finish high school? Own a home? Pursue higher education? Own a business?

When the majority of our citizens are members of a minority community that is underserved, this becomes a serious national problem that should be worked on with the same urgency as our most pressing domestic concerns. The problem is fundamentally an outgrowth of a system that lacks educational opportunities and access to capital for fledgling entrepreneurs. Where there is lack in education in one area, there is bound to be in others. So while the lack of quality education is seen in the K-12 schools that serve mostly minority students, there is also a lack of financial literacy in the homes of these working class families.

An advocacy organization I worked closely with, the Greenlining Institute, has an excellent report on this subject that explains how the financial crisis affected communities of color.

"The financial crisis devastated communities across the nation and disproportionately harmed low-income communities and communities of color. To help address this, section 342 of the Dodd-Frank Wall Street Reform and Consumer Protection Act created Offices of Minority and Women Inclusion (OMWIs) at 20 federal financial regulatory agencies."

Much of the information on the Great Recession looks at how hard the already entrenched poor and low-income communities were hit, and it is true that the single hardest hit group is low-income individuals and families. However, it is a disservice to the issue to forget to mention the fact that the minority groups in this country are disproportionately poor. Here is why this is problematic: As Dartmouth professor Leonard Greenhalgh puts it, "America needs all its citizens making their best contributions to the country's well being . . . enabling the full participation of minorities in the U.S. economy . . . It is well established that small business is the biggest source of job creation and wealth generator in the U.S., so priority needs to be given to entrepreneurship."

Breaking through the Bamboo Ceiling

The emerging reality of a growing majority that happens to be ethnic minorities, paired with the need to support small businesses in America inspired Eric and me to promote the needs of woman and minority-owned businesses across the country. If we were to truly help our generation, we would have to look twenty years down the line to know that it is the minority Millennials who would be the majority, which meant we would need to help the current ethnic minorities break through the glass ceiling, or what my community—the Asian community—calls "the bamboo ceiling." We knew that for us to really make a difference in the lives of our hometowns and for our generation, we would need to figure out how to enable the full participation of America's small businesses, and include the minority voice somewhere in the agenda. The groundwork we do today surely will affect the generations of tomorrow.

Because minorities will be the majority by 2043, if we are talking about the Millennial Generation, it is absolutely necessary to talk about minorities if we are to describe the future of America. You cannot have a future majority that is still lagging in educational attainment, entrepreneurship, and financial literacy and have it not impact our entire country. In regards to entrepreneurship, as reported above, Professor Greenhalgh believes the lack of development of minority businesses and suppliers will have dire consequences on the U.S. economy for future generations if minorities are left out of the business and workforce dialogue.

Because my career started out in supply chain, I've watched how current small business owners are operating—both minority and non-minority—and I wholeheartedly agree with Dr. Greenhalgh. We have some serious problems on the road ahead to entrepreneurial development in America. There are a myriad of challenges small businesses face in bringing their companies to the size and capacity necessary for large contracts in the government and corporate space. Some businesses argue that they are fine staying a mom n' pop size, however, it is important that minority entrepreneurs remain engaged in businesses that can employ many Americans and generate tax revenue for our country.

Unfortunately, to do this, it requires a diverse set of skill sets that are not readily available to the general public, and tends to require support of a formal education and beyond.

Because minorities tend to already lag in formal educational attainment, how far behind does it leave this future majority in developing as successful entrepreneurs? While some of the Asian subpopulations have high educational attainment and there are significant differences between the different minority populations, the scope of this work does not lend itself to sorting through this variation and its cause and effect. The point remains that the underrepresentation of any group will become a problem even more so than now as the demographics of The United States change to become more diverse.

In this excerpt below, Dr. Greenhalgh describes in his publication, *Minority Business Success,* some of the challenges America faces ahead:

"Minorities are well on their way to becoming the majority of our workforce and our entrepreneurial economy. It's well established that small business is the biggest source of job creation and wealth generation to the U.S. economy; Therefore, priority needs to be given to support entrepreneurship . . . The emphasis needs to be on development of minority businesses, of which capitalization is just one element. Successful development involves comprehensive, integrated sets of interventions. Piecemeal solutions have never worked."

The number one excuse I've heard from young people as to why they do not want to start a business is that they have no start-up capital. OK, obtaining start-up capital it requires some financial literacy, but the "comprehensive, integrated sets of interventions" necessary that he speaks of are complex, and go beyond access to capital. To properly prepare future business leaders, we must have training in what Greenhalgh calls "global-best-in-class supply-management strategy."

That means there is much more work to do beyond just financial literacy. We must not only train financially literate young people, but we must engage them in entrepreneurship, *and* they must choose to enter industries that help ensure America has a proper competitive edge in the global marketplace. An emphasis on making sure minorities are trained in these specific areas is essential in contributing to the development of the *whole* Millennial Generation's economic future. That's a lot of work, folks.

Where are Millennials supposed to get this training? How do we even know what industries to enter? How do we play catch up in this so-called "long recovery?" What do we do with America's future leaders to prepare them for the international marketplace? How can a young person grow a business to scale when very little financial literacy is being taught in America's education system? If you can't balance your personal checkbook, how are you supposed to produce a proper profit-and-loss sheet for your business?

In October 2011, I was invited to testify before Congress to discuss the lack of subcontracting opportunities for minority- and women-owned companies that were bidding on federal contracts. These business owners were the parents of my peers in the Millennial generation. And my god, were they struggling. The federal government procures billions of dollars' worth of goods and services a year—they are in fact the largest buyer in the world. Our firm, the E&J Commission, wanted to provide a voice for the growing number of diverse businesses that were entering the marketplace, so we did just that. Anyone who has ever been to D.C. knows that there is an incredible amount of paperwork and red tape one must go through to get anything done. Contracting was no different. So, our clients relied on us to help them navigate through the bureaucratic alphabet soup of governmental agencies in D.C. to try to get them to program officers and the office of small and disadvantaged business utilization (OSDBU) offices, which had a mandate to help these kinds of companies.

What was different for minorities than for other suppliers was that, if they were behind in education attainment, financial literacy, and access to capital, then surely, minorities would be behind in entrepreneurship.

Access for Women and Minorities

The E & J Commission prided itself in representing disadvantaged business communities by researching contracts available for small, disadvantaged businesses and assisting them with business development consultation. In my former capacity as Executive Director of the National Council of Asian American Business Associations, and in my former position as intern to Congressman Mike Honda, who was the Chair of the Congressional Asian Pacific American Caucus at the time, I was exposed to a number of small business owners across America who would voice their challenges within both commercial and government contracting. This is why Eric and I decided to create a social entrepreneurship initiative to assist some of the best and brightest minority and woman-owned companies in this space—so we could help them in understanding the nuances of this industry. Entering the federal market is one of the most challenging areas to break into as a small business owner, but even more so if cultural and linguistic barriers prevent one from being able to understand the complexities of government systems. So, after ten years of working with communities of color, I wanted find out what corporate leaders thought of America's future majority.

One of my mentors and dear friends through my career is a woman named Sonya Dukes. I had met her when she became Senior Vice President of Wells Fargo Bank back when I was in college. She taught me the importance of marketing and packaging a brand, how to put together a corporate proposal and business plan, and even provided seed money for my training programs so that underserved communities could learn the technical skills to running a successful enterprise.

Now a private business owner herself and co-owner of ITP Consulting, a marketing consulting firm, I wanted to get her perspective on the next generation and entrepreneurship, financial literacy and corporate careers. She said this:

> I believe the focus for the future should be the emerging entrepreneurs/Millennial/Generation Y. . . . .We are very much aware of businesses that expand beyond that age group, and there has been a lot of focus—programs, guidelines, practices, support groups—for more established business owners. More and more college graduates and high school graduates are planning their careers around entrepreneurship. The days of looking forward to a big corporate job is not as attractive as it once was, and the innovation, creativity, freedom, flexibility, empowerment to be self-defined and artistic with their talents is more appealing.

It's unreal to think 18–35 year olds will sit through a long conference of speeches and expos conducted by industry leaders twice their age and find it a productive way to spend their time. That generation lives, thinks, behaves, creates and expresses themselves in a new way, and it's full of life and energy that needs to be welcomed and engaged. We can't expect them to naturally fit into a system of structure, protocol, seniority, politics, semantics, and senseless meetings when they know they can contribute in a more effective manner from their passion and power position. We are not looking at ways to have them at the table to help stabilize the problems that exist today and that they will inherit tomorrow. It's sad that we are still viewing them as the intern/entry level/individual contributor—we're missing out on so much.

I recently experienced a major corporation establishing their first social media executive and team. I was completely disappointed when I learned they moved an inexperienced executive (50+) into the position and then built the senior team with folks 40+ in age to establish the strategy for market growth under social media. The interesting thing: they were targeting 18–35 year olds. This is just one example of being out of touch with reality, the low level positions they filled had some 30+ year olds, but they were not in the roles of influence to effect change.

There are so many stories out there, and it just shows how naive people can be when it comes to the importance and vital role of Millennials. I wonder how many major corporations and businesses pitch their services to this group; it is usually the other way around. The Millennials are trying to prove themselves to Corporate America. When that paradigm shift happens, then we'll begin to see change.

As for the financial literacy topic, I don't know how affective that topic is for anyone who doesn't have the money to manage. Unemployment and living paycheck-to-paycheck is real, so when that topic is pushed by financial services and others who feel it's the new buzzword to draw in customers and define value—it's ridiculous. The conversation needs to start with how to find access to income and balance the debt to income ratio. That's a real issue for so many people. And for the average college graduate, it's an overwhelming position to be in at such a young age. We are seeing higher rates of alcohol abuse, drug abuse, suicide, depression and other health issues. Money can make or break a person.

Women still tend to be a key market for consumer consumption and buying power, so the focus on marketing and engaging them will always be a priority. I don't, however, believe the same for minorities. A lot of corporations and businesses are moving to a new concept called "General Marketing Strategies," and for some, it means no longer segmenting each group for marketing strategies but putting them all together and using the same strategy for all groups. This can hinder the reach and support allocated to each segmented group. For example, sponsorships to organizations and institutions that specifically support ethnic groups will shift, the dollars will be distributed differently and, in some cases, decreased or eliminated.

It's a moving target, and now that we have Millennials in the mix, it will probably be a more complicated and slower process for change.

What Sonya said rang true for my friends, family members and for me, personally. These issues, among many others, inspired me to get active in the national discourse. It brought me to the Federal Reserve in the fall of 2012. I met Chairman Ben Bernanke with a group of grassroots organizers. The intense energy of a very powerful man came face to face with the intense anger Main Street was feeling because of the turbulent environment the middle class was facing amidst growing income inequality in America.

Transitioning Careers

The meeting? You wanted to know about the meeting with the Chairman. Well, it was about as exciting as the history of dinosaurs. I was so heated about the lack of empathy, concern, and response to our comments of dire straits; I lashed out in anger when I came home to Main Street about the not-so-special meeting with the Chairman of the Federal Reserve. If it wasn't the financial regulatory agencies fault, then it was Congress. When you asked Congress whose responsibility it was, they'd say the President. The President would point to a do-nothing-Congress, then, the cycle would continue.

Although understanding of my anger, I knew it was not the right response. Did the issues hit too close to home because I had experienced foreclosure? Was I getting too enmeshed in the sorrows of Main Street's stories of financial burden and unemployment? They weren't my problems, why was I getting so involved?

But they were my problems. Anyone with a compassionate heart will know, we do not achieve our success alone, and it takes the efforts of our entire community, and in fact—our entire nation—to create the environment in which individuals and businesses can thrive.

I couldn't just stand back and take an observer's point of view. I wanted to get in on the action and speak from a more authentic place, aside from ranting off statistical data and anecdotal stories that everyday Americans were telling me. I wanted to truly know what young people were going through. At that point, I wanted to hang it all up with my role in politics because I found it ineffective and too quarrelsome at the time.

Most people think, if you are passionate about something, it means you should stay in the industry. I don't believe that is necessarily true. And if it is, you have to see what part of the job you are passionate about. In the same way, I thought advocacy work and politics was my calling because I was passionate about it. But when I broke down scenarios in which I worked in both those sectors, I realized it wasn't the fighting for people's rights portion that I liked in advocacy. It wasn't the back and forth discussions between two parties that I liked. It was the helping people portion.

I would have such passionate discussions about wanting to alleviate the suffering of others that I didn't realize that my unrelenting pursuit made me suffer. Once I walked down that road, I realized there are parts of the job I did enjoy, but there are parts of it that made me physically sick—hosting event after event, meeting after meeting with the majority of the people I was serving that frankly just wanted more money and power for their own ego-needs.

I was not created to fight. The industry of politics was made to always have an opposition, which meant, I was always fighting someone or something. I also realized the parts of my job that I really liked were the parts where I was making people happy. I was measured by my success purely in numbers and the bottom line, even though I knew in my heart that I should measure my success by how happy it made people. I wanted to find a career that made people happy, and made me happy, instead of constantly struggling or fighting something.

One other clue that I was not in the right business? I was constantly exhausted.

Ariana Huffington, co-founder and editor-in-chief of the Huffington Post Media Group, wrote a book titled, *Thrive: The Third Metric to Redefining Success and Creating a Life of Well-Being, Wisdom, and Wonder*. In it, she shares a personal account of having an underlying medical problem brought on by exhaustion and lack of sleep. This story reminded me of the battles my mother took on for community; battles that made her body weak and compromised her health.

In Huffington's writings she says, "As more and more people are coming to realize, there is far more to living a truly successful life than just earning a bigger salary and capturing a corner office. Our relentless pursuit of the two traditional metrics of success—money and power— has led to an epidemic of burnout and stress-related illnesses, and an erosion in the quality of our relationships, family life, and, ironically, our careers. In being connected to the world 24/7, we're losing our connection to what truly matters. Our current definition of success is, as *Thrive* shows, literally killing us. We need a new way forward."

Ms. Huffington was absolutely right. And my exhausted was exhausted. My tired was tired. Uncertain of what the future held for me, yet unafraid to change, I found the courage to pack my bags, picked up a pen and paper, and headed to Paradise.

CHAPTER 7

Hawai'i 2013: The Experiment

"It is not in the stars to hold our destiny. It is in ourselves."
—William Shakespeare

I t was six years since the recession began. I rebuilt most of my life since then. Despite the challenges I had to overcome, I did find myself in a relatively comfortable financial space compared to my peer group. But the money was not enough. If the recession had taught me anything, it was that our societal obsession with consuming, owning, and monetizing every system possible is what got us into the mess we were in as a country in the first place. If living in D.C. taught me anything, it was that we can legislate all day, increase the national GDP, build multi-national corporations and be one of the most dominant countries in the world economy. But if a society—which is a group of individuals—doesn't encourage changing the personal habits and lifestyles of each person in that society, then our culture doesn't change.

I had an epiphany: If I truly wanted to change the system, if I really wanted to help my generation, I was going to have to start with me. I wanted to authentically connect back to myself, as well. I had lost that relationship with the most important person—me. And I don't mean that in a vain way. I mean that if I were going to be an advocate for any of these issues I cared so much about in regards to my generation—education, healthcare, small business, job creation, my parent's retirement, housing, etc.—who would take care of number one while I was taking care of the world's needs? If I were to be the vessel to carry out this work, wasn't it important that I had a relationship with myself and that I took care of myself? Wouldn't it be important that I focus on my health—focused on what kind of fuel I was putting into my body through nutritious food, diet and exercise? Wouldn't it be important to center myself, clear my mind, observe, and be in thoughtful awareness so that I could leave room to think about more complex issues of society? I had some serious work to do, and it required nothing but my body, my mind and my spirit. I was in control of the agenda. But that meant I was the only one that could stop the positive growth in my personal transformation. I was literally my own worst enemy or my number one advocate.

The best way I could think of refocusing my life mission was to get back to basics. And that started with living with very basic needs—a concept that was foreign to me. Growing up in L.A. culture, consumption was the name of the game. And although money is not necessarily a bad thing, my relationship to it and obsession with it is was what hurt me the most. Akin to an addict, I couldn't put the crack pipe down—and that crack pipe was my love for things.

So, what did I do? I weaned myself off it. I was to live on a minimum wage salary, with no car, and no family resources or my political or corporate network to be a crutch to feed my need for material things. *Work to own things. Own things so you must work.* It was a cycle that had to end. I figured that if I were to actually do this, the only place I could possibly endure it was on a beach with beautiful sunsets. A place where there are no big shopping malls, very few commercial centers to spend money, a place where nature is more of a luxury than an edifice with storefronts.

I chose one of the most enchanting, beautiful and most geographically remote places in the world—farthest from the nearest land mass than any island chain in the world; a place where land was born five million years ago. I chose the one island with an active volcano in a chain of the eight islands—the Big Island of Hawai'i.

In a place where so much history has its contrasts, Hawai'i has seen its share of violence and serenity, war and peace, eruption of volcanoes and tranquil waters. I too had a share of contrasts going on internally—I was constantly growing in my connection to myself and to a Supreme Being (of whatever name you'd like to call this Energy Force); yet I was still so attached to what some in my generation and I were accustomed to: material wealth, titles, prestige, and the things of this world.

Relinquishing my attachment to my material possessions was the first line of business. I put all my belongings in storage, I left my dog with a friend who happened to own a pet-sitting company, and I took off alone with a suitcase and one carry-on luggage.

A part of this experience also meant I was not supposed to take much money with me. My parents had purchased a one-way plane ticket for me, and I had a total of $200 to last me until I found a job. I was fairly certain, with my skill-set and abilities, I'd be able to find a job on my own merit. But to be completely honest, I was pretty naïve about how difficult this was going to be. I thought it would be a little uncomfortable, but I didn't realize it would actually twist my soul and bring the psychological turmoil that it ended up bringing. It was Hawai'i, right? It couldn't be that bad.

The room I stayed in was modest, to say the least, in comparison to my room in Los Angeles. I had a whole studio apartment to myself in L.A., with expensive furniture and comfortable bedding. Now I had a 200 square foot, white-walled room, a balcony facing a tree, and a mattress on the floor. To top it off, there was no air-conditioning in 90-degree tropical weather. Apparently, the room I was staying in had visits from a now-homeless person, who was previously renting there before being evicted; jumping the *lanai* regularly to try to sleep in his old room. He would occupy the room without permission from the landlord. You could tell he had been drinking in there, as the smell of alcohol stung through my nostrils upon arrival. Between the creaking ceiling fan, the closed windows, and the bright fluorescent light, it felt what I imagine an interrogation room to feel like.

Okay, so it wasn't the Ritz Carlton, but it was a room, and it was a bed, and it was shelter—in Hawai'i. I wasn't even 24 hours into my experiment and my high maintenance-ass was already judging coming out to Hawai'i to relinquish my material needs; when the point *was* to live like this. It took me forever to get over the fact that I didn't have a bed frame for my mattress.

Then humility struck me like a bolt of lightning. *There are people who don't even have mattresses to sleep on*, I thought to myself. *Suck it up, Princess.*

Hawai'i: 1 Jamie: 0

Despite my lack of comfort my first night, something deeper inside me made it feel like a tsunami of love had swept me up and washed me onto the shores of Hawai'i.

My first morning in Kona, I watched the birds eat breakfast perched on a branch decorated with luscious red berries. Although I was physically alone, it reminded me that, if the universe takes care of my little flying friends, surely it will take care of me.

Because my travels left me devoid of people I knew, and I hadn't made friends yet, I quickly became acquainted with my natural surroundings. Nature has provided me an abundance of company in a way I had not appreciated before. I was supercharged through dancing mosquitoes, the sound of chirping birds, beautiful music, vibrant trees, neon green geckos, buzzing bumblebees, beautiful blooming pink flowers, and the tropical greenery that is uniquely Hawai'i.

Locals vs. Tourists

As I explored the island my first few days, strangers at coffee shops, restaurants, or those simply strolling down the main downtown street of Ali'i Drive would look at me curiously and say, "Do I know you from somewhere?"

Or they would say, "Are you from here?"

It was the first place I had ever been to that I was immediately mistaken for a local. I didn't speak Pidgin, and I certainly was not familiar with local Hawaiian culture. I still felt like a tourist. But maybe it was because of my dark hair, tanned skin and Asian features that they thought I was from the Big Island. Either way, it was a very interesting experience for me because I felt like a fish out of water, when all the fish kept telling me, "Welcome home, sistah!"

Still not knowing where the local food joints were, I stopped in like a typical tourist to an oceanfront, over-priced restaurant. I began to observe all the people working. The server was a Caucasian young man, with a backwards cap, Oakley sunglasses and bleached blonde long hair. You could see the fresh sand stuck to his arm and see the crispness of his sunburn as he walked by. You could tell he had just gone surfing. His surfer friends stopped by, surfboards in tow, to chat with him. So as he leaned against the rail to entertain his friends, I people-watched as I waited for him to take my order. I looked to the left of me, and there was an older woman, who looked to be Filipina, bussing a big bucket full of dishes off to the side. She had a joyful presence about her. Hair tattered, wrinkles deep—especially around the mouth where one would smile. She struggled to carry the bucket, with no one around her helping her up the stairs. I then noticed another gentleman who looked like a cook of some sort, with sweat dripping from his face. Tired and unsettled, he looked like he had been roasting in the kitchen. He took his arm to his brow to wipe his sweat, as he was telling the other wait staff that they were out of a certain ingredient and would no longer be cooking a dish for the day. He too, looked like a Filipino. His awkward presence and facial expression of uncertainty around him, made me think he was not comfortable with the front-of-house aspects of the restaurant. This led me to believe he was a back-of-house employee, not wanting to interrupt the tourists eating, not wanting to be seen.

I was interrupted from my people watching because my server wanted to finally take my order.

"Aloha. What can I get you today?"

I glanced at the menu. Some of the "local" dishes had influences of Filipino food. They listed *lumpia*, which is a Filipino eggroll. They served it with macaroni salad and rice in true Hawaiian fashion. I had never seen food of my heritage listed in a mainstream American restaurant.

"I'll have your eggroll entrée, please."

Later that day, I stopped in to a used bookstore to see if I could find information about the influence of my heritage in Hawai'i. It turned out that a book I picked up, titled *Filipinos in Hawai'i,* highlighted the fact that nearly one in four persons in Hawai'i is of Filipino heritage. Clearly, my experience of seeing Filipino food on an American restaurant menu was a reflection of the influence Filipinos have had on the state; however, there were still problems plaguing my people.

The introduction of the book explained, "The fiction of the Aloha State masks the following facts: despite the material gains that individuals have made and used as measures of success against everyone else, Filipinos, as one of the largest populations on the islands, along with Native Hawaiians and Samoans, were vastly underrepresented in management and professional ranks while overrepresented in blue-collar sectors of production, transportation and service industries as food processors, truck drivers, seamstresses, laborers, retail workers and hotel staff."

I remembered the little old woman and the *manong* from back-of-house. They were exactly that—back-of-house. They were the backbone of the restaurants, hotels, service and agricultural industry, but nowhere to be found in the front-of-house operations. They were hidden away as line cooks, dishwashers, farm workers and living off minimum wage.

As I explored the book further, it talked of Filipino influence on the islands. "Filipinos have been in Hawai'i for more than a century, turning the rough and raw materials of sugar and pineapple into billion-dollar commodities. This book traces a history from 1946—the last year the *sakadas* (plantation workers) were imported from the Philippines—to the centennial year of their settlement in Hawai'i. Filipinos are central in much that has been built and cherished in the state, including the agricultural industry, tourism, military presence, labor movements, community activism, politics, education, entertainment and sports."

What happened to my people, the Filipinos? And what of the Native Hawaiian people? Why were they not making the economic gains of the land when they inhabited it for centuries? As I read further, the Native Hawaiians of the island had endured quite a history. From the colonization of the West, to the death of Captain Cook and the overthrow of the last Queen of the Hawaiian Kingdom, Queen Lili'uokalani, the melting pot that Hawai'i is today has a key characteristic: mixed race groups continue to grow in size while the longstanding existence of racial tension still kindles a range of emotion for the citizens of the state.

In a book titled *The Price of Paradise*, author Randall W. Roth says of Hawai'i, "We are facing social problems created by an economy that employs a large number of less-educated immigrants and newcomers in the tourist industry, who often work more than one job for wages on the low end of the pay scale. This economic situation leaves a younger generation unsupervised while parents and older siblings work longer hours to make ends meet."

All of this intrigued me. I was in a position as a young Filipina American watching both my generation and those of my heritage face the same problem: they were America's poor. I had never seen it in this light.

Walking Seven Miles to Humility

I had no Internet, so everyday, I walked to Starbucks. There, I would apply for jobs through Craigslist, Monster, and other job posting sites.

My mom had called me my second day on the island.

"Are you okay, baby girl?"

"Yeah, I'm fine. But my room is small, I don't have a car, and I have no Internet."

So there, my mother suggested that I call a family friend to borrow a car. Luckily, our family friend had one on deck. It was a modest car, but it was not working very well. Some days, when I would turn the ignition, it would start. Other days, it was rough.

After two weeks of filling out applications, I finally received a call for a restaurant position. I was looking to be a server at a restaurant, but I had never even carried a tray. I naïvely thought that pouring my cup of coffee in the morning and preparing my breakfast qualified as "food and beverage experience." My background in politics had no value to this industry.

I drove to my 1:00 P.M. interview in the loaner car. The gentleman who interviewed me had a pleasant Southern drawl and was hospitable. It was no wonder he was in the industry. He said my expertise looked good in marketing more so than in food and beverage.

I took that to mean that I was not qualified for the position. I walked slowly to the car, still licking my wounds. I stuck the key into the ignition.

It didn't start.

I took the key out, stuck it back in, tried again with no success and took it out once again.

No luck.

At this point, I had no money, no job, and no car to get to my interviews in the first place. The closest relative lived 3,000 miles away in California, and I had made only three acquaintances in my first few weeks.

I had befriended my neighbor who lived downstairs, and remembered I had stored his number a few nights before in my cell phone. He didn't pick up the first time, but then, he called back.

"Hi, Jamie, I'm in Hilo. I had to drop off a delivery. I'm sorry I can't pick you up."

The other person I called was our family friend (who I fondly call "Uncle") who loaned me the car. He was unavailable, as well.

"Uncle!" I frantically said. "The car won't start."

"I'm still at work and won't be available for the next four hours," he replied.

I told him I was going to walk. I was at the furthest end of the main street in Kona, and I had to make it all the way to the other end. Let's just say, I wasn't dressed so appropriately. In my interview dress and my high heels, I began to walk the seven miles back home.

My uncle said he was going to send for a mechanic. The problem was, my phone died. There was no way the mechanic could reach me.

Six miles later, blisters forming and sweat pouring, and limping because my shoes were inadequate for the trek, I remembered the older woman I had seen at that tourist restaurant, struggling to carry the bucket of dishes up the stairs. I was happy, at that moment, to even have the mobility to walk as far as I did. *I walked seven miles to humility.*

As the sweat came down my face, I remembered the local line cook who wiped the sweat from his brow. Despite harsh weather, some of the locals on this island were forced to deal with it. *I walked seven miles to humility.*

As I saw the beautiful Hawaiian sun, I became intensely grateful to be immersed in one of the most beautiful places in the planet, despite having no money and experiencing rather challenging circumstances. As a designated poverty-stricken county, Hawai'i had locals on the island who suffered through low wages and lifestyles far more trying than my experience at the time. I was only getting a brief glimpse of what their life was like, and I had the nerve to complain. *I walked seven miles to humility.*

A very interesting thing happened once I was mindful of my negative way of thinking: my situation immediately changed. A wave of compassion and gratitude overwhelmed my senses. I felt a serene energy come over me. I usually would throw a fit, but none of that happened. By the sixth mile, I decided to find a rock by the beach and perch myself on it to watch the surfers.

I decided to enjoy the smell of the salty sea. I decided to eat a banana from the tree, smile at the waves, and chose to bask in the Hawaiian sun, and in the peace and grace I had finally received.

The New American Dream

I continued to immerse myself in Nature. With very few friends on the island, She had become my best friend. As I sat out in the tropical garden, I felt like the wisdom of the trees was speaking to me. The aroma of jasmine and fresh rain dripping from the tips of leaves whispered to me. The rhythmic sounds of birds chirping and the rooster crowing while I gazed at the vibrant tropical plants told me something.

"What is it?" I asked.

I sat in reflective meditation. I let the volcano rock, tropical trees and sweet humid air speak to my heart:

In the seeming chaos of the world, a constant exists. In the confusion and turmoil, there is stillness and peace. In the fear and pain, there is simplicity and joy. Come away, with us, sister. We will teach you our ways. Slow down. Listen to the rhythm of our lives. We come and go, but we have been here long before you. You are born of nature, and you return to nature when the end of life calls. Our knowledge is deeper than your society will admit. Dance in new energy, bask in our warmth. We shall provide you rest under our branches, our sand and our rock.

So, I was either crazy, or I had communed with Nature and found peace in a way I never thought possible. I didn't really care which it was though, because I found happiness; true peace and joy, unfettered by the superficial. It didn't require money. It didn't require name brands, labels, a network, a car or a house. It required deep, reflective space. It required room to breathe in and out. It required present moment awareness. Stillness in my heart, feeling the warm breeze and salty water soak in my skin, made heaven available to me at any given moment of mindfulness. Not only that, I had a short glimpse of what America's entrenched poor was going through, and as someone who is a part of the generation of America's New Poor, I was motivated to find a way to tell the narrative of growing income inequality in America—but to do it in a way that also promoted this newfound peace.

I was living a new American Dream. I had found my heart and purpose in a place that had very little material wealth, but offered the *aloha* spirit of serenity and grace inspired by the Native Hawaiian

Goddess Pele. It is said in Hawaiian mythology that Pele rules in her kingdom fire pit called Halema'uma'u crater, at the summit caldera of Kilauea—one of the Earth's most active volcanoes. Many of my meditations took place just miles from Pele's home of Kilauea, and I felt a deep connection to this archetype. Her domain encompassed all volcanic activity on the Big Island, and her creative power, passion, purpose, and profound love filled my soul. I believe it was her speaking to me in that reflective moment. As if I were a diamond in the rough, Pele asked me to go through the fire so she could burn off the excess baggage and beliefs holding me back from my purpose.

What else did Pele leave me in that meditation? She left me a blueprint for this generation to live out a 2.0 version of the American Dream—one that has been repeated and said in many different ways in different times and places in history, but one that needs a new generation to remember, so that we can be, what Gandhi said, "The change we wish to see in the world."

The Millennial Blueprint I see is this: **In order to transform the societal mind (education), body (government), and spirit (community), one must focus on transforming his or her *personal* mind, body and spirit to channel one's true purpose in the world.**

The Fire Goddess had ignited my heart with this insight, and created a spark that motivated me into action. She awakened me to my own divine inspiration.

Changing the world starts with YOU, dear Millennial—the most important part of this entire story. You, the formidable force in the next chapter of American history, must find your passion and tell your story, the way I have told mine. May the Fire Goddess Pele bless you with the same strength and metaphorical fire she granted me for the journey to find my passion . . . *Godess*speed.

Pele, Goddess of Fire and Change
Help me find the spark in myself.
Help me light and fan the flames of my true desire.
Help me find my resolve and inner knowing.
Mahalo nui, Tutu Pele.

Afterword

"I would rather be ashes than dust! I would rather that my spark should burn out in a brilliant blaze than it should be stifled by dry-rot. I would rather be a superb meteor, every atom of me in magnificent glow, than a sleepy and permanent planet. The function of man is to live, not to exist. I shall not waste my days trying to prolong them. I shall use my time."

—Jack London

How?

Having just read this book, that is what I would be thinking. I get it. We need to personally be responsible for changing the world through changing ourselves. Cool. Easier said than done, though. How can I possibly change my situation or change anything going on in the world? After the insights I gained on my trip to Hawai'i, I've developed a **Six-Step Millennial Blueprint** I believe can get us going in the right direction that addresses the mind, body, and spirit balance we need to cultivate in our personal lives. By doing this, then we can go out into the world and be more effective leaders to change all the various challenges ahead of us. Anyone can do it, but it starts with your commitment to both yourself and to larger society. We need more people in the world ready to get serious about becoming change leaders in all areas of life. Time is not a luxury, and we need to walk and chew gum at the same time. As change leaders of society, we need to prepare ourselves internally while going out into the world and executing our mission of solving these problems. We need to spend our days and time well at such a critical juncture in society. At a certain point, we all need to step up to the plate and admit that dress rehearsal is over. It is show time. No soldier ever goes to war without training. No professional athlete competes without preparing. We have a battle we need to win, and the first battle is within ourselves. If each of us is winning our individual battle, then a collection of individuals are winning, and all society is *is* a collection of individuals. So this means, we can change society.

Transforming our Personal Lives

Step One: MIND
Start With Self-Examination. Before looking at society's problems, we have to look at who we are in this larger system. The answer comes from looking inward. Ask yourself, am I making the decisions that give me the best chance at success? If not, do I really believe there is nothing I could do to improve my situation? Of course not, there are way too many rags-to-riches stories in America to believe that we can't do it as well, *if the circumstances are right*. The vast majority of us are made up of the same basic abilities; it is our actions that separate us, and our actions are dictated by our thoughts. Monitor your thoughts, examine how you think, then use that examination to adjust your perception so that you can choose proper actions for each situation that arises.

What we need is an extraordinary frame of mind. I mentioned earlier in the book that Steve Jobs made sure everyone at his funeral walked away with a copy of Paramahansa Yogananda's *Autobiography of a Yogi*. These are the most important people in Steve Jobs' life coming to their last interaction with the visionary man. He chooses to have them walk away with this book about spirituality and intuition. It is an understatement to say he found these influences to be critical in his life.

I, too, cannot overstate the importance of spirituality and intuition in healing and enriching my life, materially and financially, but more importantly, in helping me achieve the states of mind that I desire. This serves the world much more than fear, anxiety, and depression.

The reason successful people find it easier to stay successful and those that struggle find it easiest to maintain their difficult circumstances is about more than mere inertia. It has to do with the emotional life of human beings that are living in abundance or desperation. When you experience scraping by paycheck-to-paycheck or worse, you feel a type of fear and panic that tends to produce progressively worse decision-making.

When you're panicking—which much of our generation is in relation to their financial situation—you're unable to think about the next rational action to take.

As you can see from my memoir, I have been in the same boat as many other young people, panicking in the face of hardship. What were the times that my life was working? It was when I was able to avoid panic and thought of the next rational action I could take that would help to improve my life. People that are in calm, stable situations find it much simpler to think of the next rational step in their life—at least financially.

But, with people that are in more desperate situations, that are panicking, they tend to demonstrate erratic behavior. And this typically causes you to do the worst thing the situation would call for, instead of the most rational thing in any given situation.

And what happens when you do the worst thing the situation could call for? You *realize* it was the worst thing you could have done, then you panic about *that*. Your panic then gets exponentially worse. More panic subsequently produces more erratic behavior, and the pattern continues. In these cases, it is very important that we continually find peace in each situation before acting on the fear. Take the time to examine your thoughts, adjust your perception if you are gravitating toward fear, then act only after you have cultivated a peaceful state. From there, you can build on that to take rational and effective steps toward change.

Step Two: BODY
Take Care of Your Physical Health. Some of the more negative happenings of the world and the troublesome experiences in our personal lives can influence us to make less-than-stellar choices. Anything as mild as boredom to life's truly challenging experiences like death of a loved one or heartbreak can drive us to put toxins in our body so we can cope with the pain of life. I am not here to tell you to never do drugs, to never eat junk food or sugar, or to never smoke. I am not an absolutist when I talk about these issues. I am here to say that my research in chapter two highlights that we need some moderation in our lives. These toxins have become coping mechanisms our generation has gravitated toward when dealing with the stresses of life, and clearly it is not working. When prescription drug abuse goes up 200%, or when 50 million people worldwide die from chronic diseases associated with being overweight, we have to look at these issues seriously. Medically numbing ourselves with prescription drugs or eating our way into obesity is unsustainable and may actually cause more problems beyond health. In Christianity, they call the body "God's Temple." I look at the body as caring for a baby. Be gentle with your temple, and honor it the same way you would

if you were caring for an infant. This is a helpful way of perceiving your body so that you make it a priority. Our bodies are the vessels that carry out the wonderful work of the world. Without a fully functioning vessel, we cannot execute our purpose efficiently. The objective is to reduce the amount of toxicity in our life—including stress or toxic relationships. You know what's good for you and what is not. If you are practicing Step One and regularly self-examining, you will know if you ate too much chocolate, worked too much, drank too much liquor, didn't exercise enough, or skipped eating your vegetables. No one needs to tell you. The Voice Within will help reveal the truth.

Step Three: SPIRIT

Cultivate a Daily Practice That Centers You. So here we are in the 21st century, a collection of individuals. And what you have are a lot of young people making a lot of bad decisions, because so much desperation is present in their financial lives, personal lives, society, the world at large; the panic into less-than-ideal behavior pattern is happening every day.

The calm, centered coping necessary to deal with all the change means we have to find that very still Voice Within that can guide and direct us *consistently*.

Whatever practice you have to calm the internal storm, whether it be through prayer to God, yoga, meditation, exercise or the like, it is a remedy to all the panic that is out there. And it may be the only remedy that actually works.

From something as small as making your bed to brushing your teeth to consciously choosing what you eat; it is in this practice of present moment awareness and connecting to something bigger than ourselves that we are able to become more effective leaders in carrying out the crucial work of the world. For me personally, devoting at least 10 minutes a day to meditation has worked wonders in my life. It immediately connects me to a higher source. Connecting to a higher source also helps us find purpose beyond the here and now. We know there is something greater we are associated with, and it is our faith in this power that reminds us that the everyday mundane has far deeper meaning than what meets the eye. This deeper meaning and purpose then leads us to transforming the societal mind (education), body (government), and spirit (community).

Transforming Society

Step Four: SOCIETAL MIND-EDUCATION
Become an Enlightened Leader and Citizen Through Education. We are the most educated generation in the history of America. We see what formal education can do for a nation, but imagine what we could do if we had leaders that were educated in emotional intelligence and higher consciousness. Pairing higher consciousness principles with formal education has tremendous value. The upside to this is that we have a chance to make the Millennial legacy one in which we have altered our consciousness on what it means to be an American citizen and an enlightened leader in this generation—specifically in the area of business. Business has tremendous power over our monetary system—a system that currently is ruling many aspects of our lives, which makes the topic of financial literacy very important in education. How we spend it, who has it, how we budget it, and where it flows is dictated by the business community.

What has been lost in the professional world today is much more than jobs or technical training; we lack business leaders who enforce a deeper moral truth that the consumer at the end of a transaction and the employee they are employing are actually human beings. There is a serious need for us to educate both our public policy makers and business leaders that human beings' lives are affected by every decision and every transaction made in the marketplace. A conscious and educated leader will most likely take into account the variable of how they are affecting others because their inquiry, their desire to learn, and their ability to problem solve tends to show them a bigger picture that highlights how human beings are affected by their decisions. Formal education isn't always necessary, however, it does tend to provide training ground for learning how to have the mental agility to work through tough scenarios necessary when being a leader. Where does having a leader with higher consciousness training come in? Well, great thinkers who lead with the heart have the ability to take a deeper examination of what life means and ask the right questions about what we want for this lifetime and what we want for this world—if they are educated to ask those questions. This generation has the ability to not only have the most educated group of leaders in our country's history, but we have the ability to create a generation of leaders that knows that what we do is not nearly as important as who we are while we are doing it. With six million young people neither in school nor in the workforce, we can solve the economic woes of our nation by creating leaders that are educated in how to create their own jobs while also looking at the moral impact. Do our decisions as professional leaders chip away at the national ethos? Do they hinder the common good of the people? Do they help solve societal issues? These questions become very important to the enlightened leader.

While we have corporate and professional leaders who are already equipped with the technical knowledge on issues of entrepreneurship, financial literacy and business skills, this new crop of leaders in the Millennial generation have the opportunity to learn all this and more— but in a way that emphasizes the needs of humanity. We must have leaders that are as concerned with the well being of society as they are with their bottom-line. Profit should never mean more than the quality of life of our citizens, and we need more corporate leaders and career professionals to come into the fold who truly believe in the overall well being of their employees and their consumers.

We can create a win-win for the business community and everyday citizens. Businesses can make money *and* help change people's lives. If corporations focused on helping their consumers to thrive rather than spending majority of their energy on figuring out how to squeeze more profits out of their consumer, they would see an upward trend in customer loyalty in the long run. They might sacrifice their quarter-to-quarter earnings for a short time, but over time, they have the chance to be a more profitable business. The consumers would have the opportunity to thrive, giving them more disposable income, perhaps allowing them to buy more of the company's product or service. This effect would be much more powerful if all or a significant portion of *Fortune 500* companies did this. When the biggest companies in the world are focused on helping the citizens thrive economically, it can have a massive impact on the economic health of everyday people.

What I also believe our education has helped us with is reforming the workplace to be a more balanced environment. When we think of history, it is often the case that we think of wars, or legal changes, or other dramatic events that affect a group of people in very powerful ways. However, even more powerful than dramatic events that affect *some*, are slow, seemingly subtle changes that have an effect on everyone.

The changes that affect everyone are what I believe Millennials will be remembered for. The research and personal experiences I have had with the Millennial Generation and the companies they work for are coming together to paint a picture of a revolution occurring over our lifetime in the area of occupational experience.

Hints of what this might look like can be seen in cutting-edge industries and locales such as the tech industry in Silicon Valley— what we are seeing at Google, for example, where an employee spends a significant percentage of their time on a passion project of their choosing. High tech companies in the area are also offering high-end food from well-credentialed chefs, yoga classes, leisure activities, and the ability to exercise at work. Oh, and with women rising in leadership positions more frequently, did I mention very high quality childcare?

Where generations before ours have ushered in many changes in the technical realms of work and which genders are able to perform them, I believe the lasting legacy of Millennials will be the emotional experience of work. We don't see hard work as being inherently a virtue. It must have meaning attached, and there must be opportunities to live a balanced and well-rounded life—or we will just take off and start our own company. And we can use these companies as mechanisms to improve our lives, that of our neighbors, our community, our country, and eventually, the world. The revolution demands that we now live in a society where we have a fulfilling life *while* we are working. We don't want to find meaning after we retire. We want to find meaning in the now—the most important time there is. Our education level has helped draw on these insights, and as we continue to have more educated members of society, this holistic approach of living and participating in the marketplace will catch on.

Step Five: *SOCIETAL BODY- GOVERNMENT*

Activate Your Role as a Citizen. There are so many ways one can participate in democracy, and the first important role you can take as a citizen is to become aware of how our government is operating. From there, try to become an expert on the topic, and immerse yourself in taking actions to improve the system. You don't have to save the world, but I do believe if more citizens truly understood how government works and participated more, we wouldn't have nearly as many problems as we do today.

For me, one of the biggest challenges I believe our generation is facing is the Supreme Court Ruling on Citizens United that ruled corporations as people. This issue becomes sticky because the most recent judicial interpretation now allows for corporations to buy into political campaigns, drowning out the voices of everyday Americans who do not have the financial means to contribute unlimited spending in political campaigns like a corporation can. Money should not be speech, and human beings should have constitutional rights—not corporations. Because a corporation does not have a beating heart, a conscience or feelings, it cannot possibly execute this 6-Step Millennial Blueprint I have introduced here. A corporation cannot self-examine in Step One, it cannot take care of its physical health as prescribed in Step Two, it cannot cultivate a daily practice of centering itself as in Step Three, and it certainly cannot become an enlightened leader as mentioned in Step Four. Only a human being can do that.

If our politicians are being bribed by corporations to create whatever policy benefits their bottom-line, then we will continue to struggle as a nation. The Great Recession will not be the last, and income inequality will continue to widen.

I could list so many other policies worthwhile of your engagement, but the point is, you need to be present in the national discourse. This issue, among many other issues affected by public policy, needs young leaders like you engaged in the dialogue. Whatever issue it is that you care about, whatever larger cause you have devoted your life to, make sure you are using your voice by registering to vote, and joining movements that improve the overall quality of life for humanity. This new way of working and living needs to be shouted from the rooftops and into the halls of Congress. Our public policy makers need to know that we are looking for a more holistic way of living out our democracy. We want every aspect of our lives to be integrated and addressed. And we are going to join forces by creating a Millennial movement for change.

Step Six: SOCIETAL SPIRIT- COMMUNITY
Use Social Media as Your Voice for Change. Most relevant among all these observations, is our contribution in social media. Everyone can

agree that this is where Millennials rule the world and can have our collective voices heard. So let's use the place we are most powerful to make the change. If you have the same hope I do, if you are interested in assisting me with a job creation program that puts young people back to work (or for some, gives them a shot of having a job for the very first time), if you are interested in having an intergenerational conversation with generations that came before us to learn how we can start to have more meaningful dialogue around these issues, start with me today on my blog "My Millennial Musings" at www.jamieborromeo.com. If you are ready to join the movement online, if you are ready to change the world through your own personal transformation and development, there is a network of leaders and mentors on my website who are eager to have you join the dialogue. Your purpose is great, your help is needed. There is just one piece of the puzzle missing, and it is you.

When joining the movement with our generation, we are asking you to share your personal story. Each human life is so important, and your story sheds light on what is going on with the *whole* generation. Take to the Twittersphere, Facebook, YouTube, Instagram or blog your Millennial experience and use **#MillennialMusings** to tell your story. We want to know the victories, the failures, the triumphs and the heartache. Tell the whole, uncut, and raw truth; the stuff that is way better than reality television. Your participation is the only way the dialogue will continue on. If Millennials all over the globe are brave enough to open their heart and story to the world, we can clearly define the problems we are all facing. From there, we can create solutions, not just for our generation, but meaningful and effective solutions to improve our country and the whole world.

In America's history we have always proven that we break through with resilience, and the greatest movements in America are proof that Millennials can do it once again for our country. The Civil Rights Movement, The American Revolution, The Women's Rights Movement,

Women's Suffrage, World War I, World War II, The end of slavery, the end of segregation, and so many other examples—highlight that Millennials come from a country that is incredibly resilient. We come from a country with a rich history in overcoming struggle, and we have to consistently revisit or possibly re-learn our history at a time when so many citizens are losing hope. The next decade can change if young people like us are coming together to have an intergenerational discussion with mom, dad, grandma and grandpa on what we want the future of America to be. To have a purposeful and accurate dialogue, we must remember the brave struggle of our nation so we can lean on it when our hope wanes, because it will.

But remember, dear Millennial, we stand on the shoulders of giants—the biggest ones being the generations who came before us who gave us access to technology. Through social media, through unexplored territory and a new frontier online, technology is where we Millennials are paving the way for the revolution ahead. We are recreating the American Dream—bringing us closer byte by byte to the heart of why the great leaders of our nation fought hard and why brave young men and women in the military were and still are willing to sacrifice their lives for our shared national ethos. Our democracy and freedom to dream and be and do the things of our heart's desire is still possible if we as a generation work hard to preserve it. With the global spirit of the Millennial Generation it is still *so* possible; the world wide web has no boundaries, as we are seamlessly connected to Millennials all over the world through the internet. We truly are the first Global Generation, which means we have a united group of young people here and abroad to help us tackle these very large issues. We are not alone, and neither are they.

We used technology as our weapon for change when we helped to elect the First Black President in our nation's history. We global Millennials overcame challenges using technology with the Arab Spring.

We used technology to forge diplomacy in the U.S. State Department, and we're going to use it again to help America remember the great nation we can become again. We are realizing how much agency we really have on the platform of technology where we Millennials thrive. We are tweeting it. We have a hash tag for it. We have a picture on Instagram for it, and we even have a selfie on Facebook to prove **<u>we are changing the world.</u>**

If your hope is lost in this unpredictable future, the wisdom of some of the greatest minds, such as Shakespeare, comfort us by reminding us, "It is not in the stars to hold our destiny. It is in ourselves."

As Millennials are slowly awakening to our own power, we are realizing that the change begins with us—in our simple, humble, everyday lives. Everyone can absolutely make a difference, and every young person is so essential to the fabric of building this new American Dream.

Your existence, your voice, and your courage give me great hope. I started, and now it is your turn. What a privilege it is to tell the story with you. *Namaste, aloha, and salamat* my friends. Infinite gratitude for opening your hearts and joining the movement.

About the Author

Jamie Borromeo is a Millennial commentator with a uniquely illuminating perspective on Gen Y and its interaction with the business, political, and social spheres. She currently is the President of THE E&J COMMISSION LLC, a marketing and contract strategies firm based in Washington, D.C. She is also co-founder and CEO of GenerationDrive Entrepreneurs Network—a national non-profit that mentors young adult start-up firms. Ms. Borromeo has co-chaired the Clinton Foundation Millennium events in both New York City and Hollywood with President Clinton and Honorary Chair Chelsea Clinton to engage the next generation of leaders and philanthropists on global issues. She formerly served on the Small Business Advisory Group for the U.S. Department of Energy and was a founding member of the Democratic National Committee's Small Business Council. Borromeo was named one of "America's Top Women Mentoring Leaders" in the 2011 issue of *WOW* Magazine. She has been featured on *CNN*'s *Reliable Sources*, *NBC*, *CBS* Radio, Tedx, and *AsianWeek*. Borromeo graduated with a Bachelor of Arts Degree in Sociology from the University of California Santa Cruz, and is a graduate of the UCLA Anderson School of Management, Management Development for Entrepreneurs Program. She currently lives in Kailua-Kona on the Big Island of Hawai'i.

Citations

Preface

Radio.com. "Behind the Song: Lorde's 'Royals.'" January 7, 2014. http://radio.com/2014/01/07/behind-the-song-lordes-royals.

Metrolyrics. "Lorde Lyrics." January 7, 2014. http://www.metrolyrics.com/royals-lyrics-lorde.html.

"Top 10 Everything of 2013." *Time*. December 4, 2013. http://entertainment.time.com/2013/12/04/arts-and-entertainment/slide/top-10-songs.

Introduction

"Baby Boomer Spending Habits: Here's What's Really Hurting Their Retirement." *Forbes*. January 18, 2014. http://www.forbes.com/sites/halahtouryalai/2012/10/15/baby-boomer-spending-habits-heres-whats-really-hurting-their-retirement.

FreePatentsOnline.com. "The Labor Market in the Great Recession—An Update to September 2011." January 18, 2014. http://www.freepatentsonline.com/article/Brookings-Papers-Economic-Activity/289721596.html.

Project Syndicate. Hill, Steven. "The Mirage of Youth Unemployment." January 18, 2014. http://www.project-syndicate.org/commentary/the-mirage-of-youth-unemployment-by-steven-hill.

Chapter 1

"CPA and Former IRS Agent Offers Tips to Help Get Finances in Order." *The Acorn.* July 17, 2014. http://www.theacorn.com/news/2014-07-17/Business/CPA_and_former_IRS_agent_offers_tips_to_help_getfi.html.

Wells Fargo. "Eight in Ten Millennials Say Great Recession Taught Them to Save 'Now,' Wells Fargo Survey Finds." June 10, 2014. https://www.wellsfargo.com/press/2014/20140610_millennials.

"Every Every Every Generation Has Been the Me Me Me Generation." *The Wire.* January 9, 2014. http://www.thewire.com/national/2013/05/me-generation-time/65054.

ABC News. "Gay, Lesbian, Bisexual and Transgender Kids Struggle on the Streets." December 13, 2011. http://abcnews.go.com/Health/national-report-16-million-youth-homeless-experts-40/story?id=15147566.

Twenge, Jean. *Generation Me: Why Today's Young Americans Are More Confident, Assertive, Entitled—and More Miserable Than Ever Before.* New York: Atria Books, 2007.

Georgetown University Center on Education and the Workforce. "Failure to Launch." September 2013. http://cew.georgetown.edu/failuretolaunch.

Moyers and Company. "The Great American Class War: Plutocracy Versus Democracy." December 13, 2013. http://billmoyers.com/2013/12/13/the-great-american-class-war-plutocracy-versus-democracy.

United States Department of Labor, Bureau of Labor Statistics. "How the Government Measures Unemployment." June 2, 2014. http://www.bls.gov/cps/cps_htgm.htm.

Inequality for All. Documentary. Directed by Jacob Kornbluth. Performed by Robert Reich. Radius. 2013.

Complex. "iPresident: How Social Media Shaped the Narrative of Barack Obama." January 9, 2014. http://www.complex.com/tech/2013/01/ipresident-social-media-and-the-narrative-of-barack-obama.

"Mark Fowler (American government official)." *Encyclopædia Britannica.* January 9, 2014. http://www.britannica.com/EBchecked/topic/1577168/Mark-Fowler.

"The Media Monopoly." *Multinational Monitor.* January 9, 2014. http://www.multinationalmonitor.org/hyper/issues/1987/09/pearson.html.

Take Back Your Brain! "The Merchants of Cool." January 9, 2014. http://www.takebackyourbrain.com/2008/the-merchants-of-cool.

"Millennials Struggle with Financial Literacy." *USA Today.* April 24, 2012. http://usatoday30.usatoday.com/money/perfi/basics/story/2012-04-23/millenials-financial-knowledge/54494856/1.

Twenge, Jean. "Millennials: The Greatest Generation or the Most Narcissistic?" *The Atlantic.* May 2, 2012. http://www.theatlantic.com/national/archive/2012/05/millennials-the-greatest-generation-or-the-most-narcissistic/256638.

"Millennials: The Me Me Me Generation." *Time.* May 20, 2013. http://time.com/247/millennials-the-me-me-me-generation.

Kotkin, Joel. *The Next Hundred Million: American in 2050.* New York: Penguin, 2010.

"The Reconquest of Cool." *Adbusters.* January 9, 2014. https://www.adbusters.org/magazine/76/The_Reconquest_of_Cool.html.

ArmstrongEconomics.com. "Shadow Banking." January 9, 2014. http://armstrongeconomics.com/2013/11/30/shadow-banking.

"Shadow Banking System." *Wikipedia, The Free Encyclopedia.* January 9, 2014. http://en.wikipedia.org/wiki/Shadow_banking_system.

"Television in the United States." *Britannica Escola Online.* January 9, 2014. http://www.britannica.com/EBchecked/topic/1513870/Television-in-the-United-States.

"Who's Financially Smarter? Gen-Y Tops Boomers." *Wall Street Journal.* September 28, 2012. http://blogs.wsj.com/marketbeat/2012/09/28/whos-financially-smarter-gen-y-tops-boomers.

New Left Media. "Who's Really Waging the Class War?" January 9, 2014. http://blog.newleftmedia.com/post/70435676646/whos-really-waging-the-class-war-the-historian.

Chapter 2

LiveScience. "Battle Still Rages for Vets in College." January 18, 2014. http://www.livescience.com/16977-young-war-veterans-risky-behaviors.html.

Orsi, Robert A. *Between Heaven and Earth: The Religious Worlds People Make and the Scholars Who Study Them.* New Jersey: Princeton University Press, 2004.

Washington D.C. Center of Self-Realization Fellowship. "DC Center of SRF." January 18, 2014. http://dccentersrf.org/AboutSRF.html.

CNN. "FDA Aims to Tighten Control of Hydrocodone." January 18, 2014. http://www.cnn.com/2013/10/25/us/fda-painkiller-controls/index.html.

CBS Baltimore. "FDA Calls for Tighter Rules for Prescription Drug Use." January 18, 2014. http://baltimore.cbslocal.com/2013/10/26/fda-calls-for-tighter-rules-for-prescription-drug-use.

PBS NewsHour. "For Some Wounded Veterans, Strong Prescription Drugs Can Be Cause of More Pain." January 18, 2014. http://www.pbs.org/newshour/bb/military/july-dec13/veteransrx_12-07.html.

Technorati. "Hitting the Books Hard, with a Little Help from Adderall." January 18, 2014. http://technorati.com/women/article/hitting-the-books-hard-with-a/page-2.

Idlehearts. "If You Want to Awaken . . . ." January 18, 2014. http://www.idlehearts.com/if-you-want-to-awaken/893.

"In Their Own Words: 'Study Drugs.'" *The New York Times.* January 18, 2014. http://www.nytimes.com/interactive/2012/06/10/education/stimulants-student-voices.html.

"The Last Gift Steve Jobs Gave to Family and Friends Was a Book about Self Realization." *Seattlepi.com.* January 18, 2014. http://www.seattlepi.com/technology/businessinsider/article/The-Last-Gift-Steve-Jobs-Gave-To-Family-And-4805747.php.

"Millennial Narcissism: Helicopter Parents Are College Students' Bigger Problem." *Slate.* January 18, 2014. http://www.slate.com/articles/health_and_science/medical_examiner/2013/12/millennial_narcissism_helicopter_parents_are_college_students_bigger_problem.html.

KMOV.com, St. Louis. "Millennials Are the Most Stressed Generation, Survey Finds." January 18, 2014. http://www.kmov.com/news/editors-pick/Millennials-are-the-most-stressed-generation-survey-finds-190744871.html.

Blog.Viacom. "The Next Normal: An Unprecedented Look at Millennials Worldwide." November 15, 2012. http://blog.viacom.com/2012/11/the-next-normal-an-unprecedented-look-at-millennials-worldwide.

Yogananda, Paramahansa. *The Second Coming of Christ: The Resurrection of the Christ Within You,* xxi. Los Angeles, CA: Self-Realization Fellowship, 2004.

Associated Press. "Study: 15 Percent of US Youth Out of School, Work." January 18, 2014. http://bigstory.ap.org/article/study-15-percent-us-youth-out-school-work-0.

"What Really Shaped Steve Jobs' View of India—Realms of Intuition or the Pains of Delhi Belly?" *The Economic Times.* January 18, 2014. http://articles.economictimes.indiatimes.com/2011-10-25/news/30320340_1_delhi-belly-intuition-indian-villages.

"Why Millennials Can't Grow Up (Commentary)." *Syracuse.com.* January 18, 2014. http://www.syracuse.com/opinion/index.ssf/2013/12/why_millennials_cant_grow_up_commentary.html.

Expressions of Spirit by Will Doran. "Yoga, Why We Practice." January 18, 2014. http://www.expressionsofspirit.com/yoga/why-we-practice.htm.

Advanced Yoga Practices. "Yogi Book." January 18, 2014. http://www.aypsite.org/forum/topic.asp?TOPIC_ID=10471.

Chapter 3

NPR. "The Arab Spring: A Year of Revolution." December 17, 2011. http://www.npr.org/2011/12/17/143897126/the-arab-spring-a-year-of-revolution.

Goodreads. Quote by Malala Yousafzai: "I raise up my voice—not so I can shout but so that those without a voice can be heard." January 18, 2014. http://www.goodreads.com/quotes/850987-i-raise-up-my-voice-not-so-i-can-shout-but.

"Just How Cool Is the Pope? Wayward Millennials Flocking to Church." *New York Post.* December 12, 2013. http://nypost.com/2013/12/12/how-pope-francis-made-catholicism-cool.

"Millennials Will Soon Rule the World: But How Will They Lead?" *Forbes.* January 18, 2014. http://www.forbes.com/sites/joshbersin/2013/09/12/millenials-will-soon-rule-the-world-but-how-will-they-lead/2.

NPR. "More Young People Are Moving Away From Religion, but Why?" January 15, 2013. http://www.npr.

org/2013/01/15/169342349/more-young-people-are-moving-away-from-religion-but-why.

U.S. Department of Homeland Security. "National Terrorism Advisory System." January 9, 2014. http://www.dhs.gov/national-terrorism-advisory-system.

NBC News. "'Our Generation Is a Lost Cause': Spain's Youth Struggle to Chart a Life Amid Economic Crisis." January 18, 2014. http://worldnews.nbcnews.com/_news/2013/08/25/20022234-our-generation-is-a-lost-cause-spains-youth-struggle-to-chart-a-life-amid-economic-crisis?lite.

"Pope Francis, The People's Pope." *Time*. December 11, 2013. http://poy.time.com/2013/12/11/person-of-the-year-pope-francis-the-peoples-pope.

"The Pope: How the World Will Change." *La Repubblica*. October 1, 2013. http://www.repubblica.it/cultura/2013/10/01/news/pope_s_conversation_with_scalfari_english-67643118.

"Young and Educated in Europe, but Desperate for Jobs." *The New York Times*. January 18, 2014. http://www.nytimes.com/2013/11/16/world/europe/youth-unemployement-in-europe.html?pagewanted=all.

NPR. "Youth Protests Sweep Spain as Unemployment Soars." January 18, 2014. http://m.npr.org/story/136683688.

Chapter 4

Gallup. "Americans See Congress as Ineffective, Self-Serving, Entrenched." January 19, 2014. http://www.gallup.com/poll/141008/Americans-Congress-Ineffective-Self-Serving-Entrenched.aspx.

U.S. Department of Education. "Federal Pell Grant Program." January 19, 2014. http://www2.ed.gov/programs/fpg/index.html.

"John Steinbeck's Bitter Fruit." *The Guardian*. November 21, 2011. http://www.theguardian.com/books/2011/nov/21/melvyn-bragg-on-john-steinbeck.

Free Enterprise. "More Countries Pass U.S. by in Education Rankings." January 19, 2014. http://www.freeenterprise.com/education-workforce/more-countries-pass-us-education-rankings.

ABC News. "Politicians: Ignore the Millennial Student Loan Crisis at Your Own Risk." December 5, 2013. http://abcnews.go.com/Business/politicians-ignore-millennial-student-loan-crisis/story?id=21195661&page=2.

OECD. "The Programme for International Student Assessment." December 12, 2013. http://www.oecd.org/pisa/aboutpisa.

"Student Loans Are Becoming a Drag on the US Economy." *Time*. January 19, 2014. http://business.time.com/2013/10/18/student-loan-are-becoming-a-drag-on-the-us-economy.

NBC News. "US Teens Lag in Global Education Rankings as Asian Countries Rise to the Top." January 19, 2014. http://usnews.nbcnews.com/_news/2013/12/03/21733705-us-teens-lag-in-global-education-rankings-as-asian-countries-rise-to-the-top?lite.

ABC News. "Vote 2010 Elections: Sarah Palin Gets Potential 2012 GOP . . . ." January 19, 2014. http://abcnews.go.com/Politics/vote-2010-elections-sarah-palin-potential-2012-gop/story?id=12026196.

Chapter 5

Clinton, Bill. *Back to Work: Why We Need Smart Government for a Strong Economy*. New York: Knopf, 2012.

Echoing Green. "Be the Founder of Your Career." January 19, 2014. http://www.echoinggreen.org/blog/be-the-founder-of-your-career.

On the Issues. "Bill Clinton on Corporations." January 19, 2014. http://www.ontheissues.org/Celeb/Bill_Clinton_Corporations. htm.

Global Health Corps. "Clinton Development Initiative." January 19 2014. http://ghcorps.org/partners/our-partners/our-placement-organizations/clinton-development-initiative.

"Generation Sell." *The New York Times.* November 12, 2011. http://www.nytimes.com/2011/11/13/opinion/sunday/the-entrepreneurial-generation.html?_r=0.

"Jeremy Heimans of Purpose.com on Mobilizing Millions for Change." *Forbes.* January 19, 2014. http://www.forbes.com/sites/ rahimkanani/2011/12/13/jeremy-heimans-of-purpose-com-on-mobilizing-millions-for-change.

Heimans, Jeremy. "Join the Insurgency Against the Jobs Crisis." *Huffington Post.* January 19, 2014. http://www.huffingtonpost. com/jeremy-heimans/jobs-crisis-insurgency_b_1871271.html.

Idealist. "Purpose." January 19, 2014. http://www.idealist.org/view/ org/tTBpP5bMjPw4.

National Resources Defense Council. "Social Entrepreneurship: How Millennials Can Be the Next Greatest Generation." January 19, 2014. http://switchboard.nrdc.org/blogs/dmurray/social_ entrepreneurship_how_mi.html.

"What Millennials Want Most: A Career That Actually Matters." *Forbes.* January 19, 2014. http://www.forbes.com/sites/ forbesleadershipforum/2012/07/03/what-millennials-want-most-a-career-that-actually-matters.

Entrepreneur. "Why Americans Love Small Business." January 19, 2014. http://www.entrepreneur.com/article/226176.

Chapter 6

Greenhalgh, Leonard. *Minority Business Success: Refocusing on the American Dream.* California: Stanford Press, 2011.

The Greenlining Institute. "Strengthening the Financial Sector Through Diversity." August 20, 2013. http://greenlining.org/issues/2013/omwi-ref-report.

Huffington, Ariana. *Thrive: The Third Metric to Redefining Success and Creating a Life of Well-Being, Wisdom, and Wonder.* New York: Harmony, 2014.

Chapter 7

Goddess Wisdom. "Awakening the Goddess Within." May 12, 2013. http://awakeningthegoddesswithin.net/featured-goddess-pele/

Filipinos in Hawai'i Project. "Filipinos in Hawai'i." January 12, 2014. http://filipinosinhawaii.info/about-the-book.php.

Roth, Randall W. *The Price of Paradise, Vol. II.* Hawaii: Mutual Publishing, 1993.